RUN THROUGH BARRIERS

How overcoming obstacles to running will transform your health, boost your energy, and rewind your fitness age.

Clint Adam Lovell

CONTENTS

MEDICAL DISCLAIMER

This book does not provide medical advice. All information, including but not limited to, text, graphics, images and other material contained within this book are for informational purposes only. No material in this book is intended to be a substitute for professional medical advice, diagnosis or treatment. Always seek the advice of your physician or other qualified health care provider with any questions you may have regarding a medical condition or treatment and before undertaking any exercise, and never disregard professional medical advice because of something you have read in this book.

PREFACE

October 2011

I'm only one mile into my first run in over five years, and I feel terrible. Every step is making my lungs heave in rebellion. I plod on to eventually rack up another mile at a slow pace. Purple in the face, I head back home. I didn't know it at the time, but this run had just rekindled a small ember of motivation that would ignite a decade of physical discovery.

INTRODUCTION

Running is medicine. This is something I'm sure about. It can boost your physical and mental health, reduce stress and improve your overall wellbeing.

So why isn't everyone running all the time?

Simply put, it is the obstacles that we build up. Physical health, mental health, stress, busyness, tiredness – all these things can be massive barriers to enjoying the benefits that exercise can bring. And it is one of life's ironies that the things that keep us from exercising are often the things that would be made much better by it.

In my own life, I have experienced extreme anxiety and panic attacks since the age of 16. These have ebbed and flowed over the years from being completely controlling to being more of a background presence. I have also fallen into physical ruts, where I have let my fitness slump and become stuck in a downward spiral of tiredness.

I know how difficult it can be to overcome some of these barriers, and I also know how transformative it can be when you do. Running isn't a cure for physical and mental challenges, but it certainly is a potent elixir. In the last ten years, running has dramatically improved all aspects of my health, and I have developed a deep interest in the physical body. This, in turn, has led me to achieve my Level 2 Fitness Instructor qualification and to studying for my Level 3 Personal Trainer and Nutritional Therapist qualifications.

In this book, you will hear the stories of people who have overcome many obstacles to achieve incredible running feats.

There's Eileen Noble, one of Britain's oldest female marathoners, who only took up running at the age of 50. We have Roger Wright, who has battled obesity to rack up over 66 marathons in 11 years. And we'll hear from Ais North, who despite being in her 70s, hasn't let heart attacks and cancer stand in the way of her ultramarathon ambitions. There's advice from busy mother Delores Durko on finding time in crammed schedules for fitness and an emotional account of how Marlene Lowe has taken on M.E. and Chronic Fatigue Syndrome to realise her fitness goals.

Through these and many more inspirational stories, you'll discover that no obstacle to running is too big to be overcome.

In the first part of the book, we'll explore simple methods that you can use to challenge, remove and replace common barriers to running with positive actions and make exercise a sustainable part of your busy life. We'll analyse the obstacles, such as ageing and unfitness, uncovering why we've been conditioned to believe these things should stop us from exercising. We'll then challenge these beliefs with truths by using real-life examples and facts to dispel the myths. Finally, we'll create motivating actions that you can use to kick-start your fitness.

The second part of the book is focused on training the body with comprehensive running plans that will take you from a complete beginner to achieving your personal running goals. There are week-by-week plans that cover 5k, 10k, and half marathon distances. And there are also more advanced plans for both the 10k and half marathon distances.

This book aims to fuel you with the inspiration you need to get started and then arm you with the knowledge you need to put it into practice. But the great thing with running is that it isn't, and should never be, complicated. All you need is yourself, your trainers, and the right mindset. Sound good? Let's get going.

PART 1 – TRAINING YOUR MIND: BARRIERS, TRUTHS, AND ACTIONS

CHAPTER 1

The age barrier: "I'm too old to run"

"You are never too old to run. If you can walk, then you can run. It's the same, but a bit quicker."

EILEEN NOBLE – UK'S OLDEST FEMALE MARATHONER

The Barrier

Finding the motivation to keep exercising as we get older isn't easy. For many people, age is one of the most significant barriers to starting running. How many times have you heard people say, "I used to run when I was younger", followed by one of any number of excuses as to why they no longer do it? If you're anything like me, lots. And like me, you may well have uttered those words yourself at some point.

As silly as it sounds, when I started putting on weight in my early 30s, I rationalised this in my mind by thinking that it was just part of ageing. I began to resign myself to the idea that my peak physical condition was behind me and that I would have to accept that my body was slowing down.

I had become stuck in a negative cycle where my inactivity made me gain weight and feel tired, which made me want to move even less. Coupled with my mind telling me that I was getting old, it was a recipe for a prematurely ageing body and a fast-track ticket to middle age.

Looking back now, I can see how ridiculous this was. I was only 33. If I could travel back in time and show myself the physical achievements I have now made, my past self would be amazed. At that point, however, if someone had suggested to me that I could run a marathon, I would have laughed in their face. The post-30 bulge had kicked in, I was past my peak, and it was inevitable.

It's this feeling of inevitability that starts to build barriers in our minds to what we can achieve. And over time, these barriers become beliefs. Beliefs that we are too old to run a marathon, cycle 100 miles, or climb a mountain.

These thoughts aren't helped by the ingrained idea within modern society that our physical best is over once we are past our

20s. As a culture, we seem to worship youth; TV, advertising, and social media are full of young 20-somethings, all at their peak. Most pop stars appear, burn bright, and then disappear before they get old. Even professional athletes typically retire in their early 30s.

Why is this? Is there any evidence to back up this perception that we are past our best at this age? Let's review some of the facts.

For starters, both men and women go through physical changes at around 30. Women experience a drop in estrogen, and men a reduction in testosterone. Both these factors can lead to the slowing of metabolisms and also weight gain[1].

Our aerobic capacity also reduces over time, with our maximum heart rate dropping 1bpm per year as we age. The average 20-year-old's heart ticks along at a sprightly maximum of 200bpm but by 30, this has already dropped to 190bpm. And by 40, it has fallen even further to 180bpm[2].

And before we're done with the bad news, we also lose muscle mass as we age. Our bodies just can't keep up the same pace of cellular regeneration that they once did, meaning muscle fibres die.

So, there is certainly some scientific evidence to back up this notion of a natural speed bump in the road to fitness by the age of 30. But don't throw this book in the bin and run to the couch in despair just yet. Next, we will see why these changes don't have to mean an end to incredible physical achievements.

The Truth

In his excellent book, Survival Of The Fittest[3], Mike Stroud argues that declining fitness as we age is a relatively modern phenomenon. This, he theorises, was mainly due to the very active lifestyles necessary for our hunter-gatherer ancestors to survive.

Effectively, if you couldn't run for your meal, you didn't eat. If you didn't eat, you didn't survive.

So, thanks to hundreds of thousands of years of evolution, our bodies have actually been conditioned to maintain a very high level of fitness right through to old age. It's only in the last 60 years that our work lives have become more sedentary, and we've been permitted the luxury of being able to move less as we age.

Mike Stroud shares the example of Helen Klein, an ultra-distance athlete who didn't even start distance running until she was 55 years old. She then went on to complete 75 marathons and 150 ultra-marathons, beating all others in her category. And this isn't an isolated incident. There are many examples of extraordinary fitness levels achieved by people in their 70s and beyond. In the course of researching this book, I came across the incredible running achievements of Eileen Noble.

At 86, Eileen is one of Britain's oldest female marathon runners, with many half marathons and marathons to her name. Similar to Helen Klein, Eileen didn't even take up running until she was in her early fifties. I was curious to find out what motivates Eileen to keep running and what challenges she has faced over the years. She was kind enough to offer the following advice to older runners.

"There were two reasons for me starting running in my early 50s. Firstly, I had always been interested in road running, and when I saw other people out running, I really wanted to give it a go. Secondly, I was also keen to do some weight-bearing exercise, as my only exercise at the time was swimming.

When I first started out, the main challenge I had to overcome was the embarrassment of being seen out running. Back then, it was nowhere near as popular as it is now, and I hardly ever saw any other female runners. I wondered where they did their training, as there were always female runners in races – although not nearly as many as males. Fortunately, I found a friend who was also keen to run and going out together made it much easier.

Running into my 80s has made me accept the fact that I am going to be really slow – I am always at the back of the field in races. Twenty years or so ago, I used to see how many people were in front of me at the finish of a race. Now, I just count how many are behind me (and hope there are some).

I stay motivated to keep running because I would miss it so much if I stopped. Also, at my age, I cannot even take a break and go back to it later. I certainly find it really hard to drag myself out of bed early on a Sunday morning to do a long training run, but I feel sure younger people have the same problem. I also really enjoy the social side, such as having coffee afterwards with my running friends.

Until a few years ago, I used to go swimming on my non-running days, and always swam quite strenuously. Unfortunately, I had to give up driving because of my poor eyesight so I rarely go swimming now. It's a bit much to walk there and back as well as swim. I have a bicycle and use that for short journeys, but I certainly wouldn't call myself a cyclist. I have done one triathlon, but it was just an entry-level one, with a pool swim.

My advice to anyone who thinks they are too old to run is that you are never too old. If you can walk, then you can run. It's the same, but a bit quicker.

A good way to start is with Parkrun, where you will be with lots of other runners of all abilities. You can jog and walk around the route really slowly to start with and hopefully improve. The atmosphere is really friendly and I hope that when I can no longer manage even 10K events, I will still be able to stagger around my local Parkrun. They take place all over the world, and I have done Parkruns in Sydney and Adelaide, as well as lots nearer to home."

At the time of writing, Eileen is already busy preparing for her next Marathon.

The interesting thing with Eileen's story is that at the age of 50, when most people are thinking of slowing down a bit, she threw herself into a whole new exercise regime. She's clocked up 19 marathons to date – not to mention half marathons and the casual reference to a triathlon. Her tenacity, passion and dedication to running are clear from her story, as is her appetite for trying new things – which could give some insight into how she maintains her youthful outlook.

Another inspiring story I came across while writing this book was that of Ais North. Ais is an enthusiastic ultramarathoner who is incredibly passionate about proving that age is no barrier to physical achievements. Having got into ultra-running in her 60s, Ais has since completed many ultramarathons and also overcome many physical obstacles. I was intrigued to find out what motivated her to begin running such long distances at an age where most people hang up their running shoes, and she was kind enough to share how she got started.

"I did not have a lightning flash or a sudden desire to start running for fitness or to lose weight – or compete in ultras. I've been fit and fairly energetic all my life. I ran when I was at school in the 1960s, achieving medals at local games for 400 and 800 yards and then the "Ladies mile" – don't get me started on inequality and running in those days – but the attitude towards female runners lead me to give up around 22. Even back then, I knew I was a distance runner, and women just didn't get to compete at the longer distances. I didn't know how to fight back or change things.

Fast-forward to 2014, and I was working in San Francisco. The hills in that glorious city beckoned me, so I started getting up at 6am and going for a walk and then a mix of walking and jogging. I was 64 and not really exercising, simply enjoying a half hour in the early mornings before work. That Christmas, our eldest daughter said that she and a friend had entered "The Race to the Stones", a 100km mixed-pace race that ran along the Ridgeway and finished in Avebury, Wilt-

shire, near where I lived. My daughter and her friend were going to walk it, so I asked if I could join them to raise money for a London hospital charity that I chaired. They agreed, and as the race was in July 2015, there was plenty of time to get walking. Around February 2015, I decided I would run and walk the 100km. I don't actually know why, other than I'm a competitive soul, and somehow walking a race didn't really fit my personality. And as I had been enjoying a bit more running at home, I thought, "why not?" That change started a journey that I'm still on.

When I entered this race, I had no real expectations other than to finish. I rarely think about doing something that I don't believe I can achieve. If I fail, I fail and learn and then move on. I'm not saying failure doesn't affect me; it does. But worrying about whether or not I can achieve something when I have no way of knowing the outcome is a waste of energy. Instead of worrying, I prepared for this race in minute detail; I researched everything, I got myself a trainer, I learnt about fuelling, I read up about shoes and socks and other kit. I was nervous with excitement but not fearful.

The sport has exploded in the last six years, but when I started back in 2014, not that many folks were running such long distances and were mostly supportive because I was raising money. A few people raised an eyebrow and said in a nice way, "You're mad!" or an equivalent. My family are super supportive. My husband is my number one fan and helps me plan every race, and our two daughters, their partners, quite a few of their friends, my mother, sisters and their families and my husband's family all support me 100%.

As someone about to run headlong into my 8th decade on planet earth, I have come to realise that I don't recover as quickly as I did when I was 35 or 45 or 55. It's just a fact and I have to recognise that after a long race, I can't run another one four weeks later. Not that I haven't tried. I did, and it resulted in a DNF at 50 miles, followed by bitter disappointment and annoyance at my stupidity.

Three things keep me motivated as I get older; mental fitness, physical fitness, and achievement. My work requires me to be sharp and decisive, and running helps with this mental alertness. The trails I run require me to think as well as run. I don't want to be sedentary in my 80s and 90s. I still want to be strong and able to run, go for walks and climb hills with my family.

As for achievement, I am still very competitive and want to improve and compete, even win in my age group or beat some younger folks. I tend to compete with myself a lot and consider that I'm winning just by being faster today than I was in 2015. To be able to run at 80, 90, 100 – fantastic. The taller the mountain, the more I want to reach the summit! I've had this ambition to enter the Ultra-Trail du Mont Blanc (UTMB) since 2017. It was at this time I realised I was getting better at ultra-running after completing the Fling Race, a 53-mile race up and around Loch Lomond on the West Highland Way in Scotland. My UTMB goal has been thwarted twice because of illness, but I still have the ambition. I just need the points, the coach and an entry ticket.

I don't meet many people that are my age that ask how to start running in later life. Most folks think I've been running for years and tend to explain why they can't run – not ask how they should start. This is sad. However, if I were to be asked, I'd most likely say that starting with a 100km race is not ideal, but don't let me stop you. I'd say start small. Dependent on how fit you believe you are – walk before you run, then introduce running into your walking. You use the whole of your body in running, so at any age, I would suggest that you incorporate some form of strength training into your life as well as something like yoga for flexibility and balance. It is very easy to injure yourself if you don't. Strengthening your body, especially the core, helps keep you upright, and that helps with your breathing and endurance as well as keeping your legs and arms moving in unison. I like trail running because it works my body differently to road running. You have to pay more attention and move over and around rocks and tree roots. This also helps strengthen parts of you that you may not have used for years, which is another reason you should incorporate specific strength training into your routine so that you don't twist badly and injure yourself.

All in all, starting to run in later years is no different than starting at any age. Try it, and if, like me, you get hooked, then that is fantastic; it is a wonderful way to enjoy your neighbourhood and countryside, get fit, and make new friends too."

It's a cliché to say that age is just a number, but what is clear is that a positive mindset can override age milestones. And this is something that Eileen and Ais have in abundance. These examples prove that age is certainly no barrier to doing the seemingly impossible when it comes to any physical challenge. If you're willing to put in the dedication, you can still be achieving things in your 70s and 80s that some people don't dare to dream of doing in their 20s.

People like Eileen and Ais have successfully rewound their biological clocks. And what most people don't realise is that they can do exactly the same. It's perfectly possible to maintain, and even build, fitness as you get older.

When it comes to exercise, we all have our chronological age, but then we also have our biological age. Using my pre-exercise self as an example – and based on my heart rate, running speed, and other measurements such as VO2 Max – I've calculated my biological age was that of an averagely fit 50-year-old when I was just 33 years old. Not great. But with ten years of regular running, I know that my physical fitness age is now equivalent to that of a fit 20-year-old.

So even when taking into account the natural effects of ageing, because my starting point was low and my endpoint high, I have effectively reversed the negative effects of inactivity. That's a whopping 30 years knocked off my fitness age in just ten years. It's no wonder that I feel more energised than ever before.

Obviously, if we use the example of a 30-year-old elite-level athlete who's at the peak of their fitness, naturally, they are going to experience a very small decline year-on-year compared to a 21-year-old athlete in their prime. But that's because they are operating at their absolute optimum. But for the majority of us, this isn't the case.

In a Runners World article on ageing, they stated that mean marathon and half-marathon times were virtually identical for non-elite athletes aged between 20 to 49[4].

One reason running is so good for reducing our fitness age is that it is a brilliant form of aerobic exercise. It works the lungs and increases our aerobic capacity. Scientists have even gone as far as to say that lung capacity, good and bad, can alter our biological age by several decades. And even though the earlier you start, the better, it really is never too late to begin. In other studies, it's been suggested that even if you begin exercising in your 80s, it can still slow and reverse the negative effects of biological ageing[5].

All this points to the fact that for the average person, our fitness is far from over as we start to age. We can turn back the clock on our biological age, we can compete with people much younger, and we can achieve incredible physical feats, as Eileen and Ais prove.

The Actions

Now we understand the natural effects of ageing on the body and how it is possible to reduce our biological age, it's time to set some of the first practical steps.

<u>Go and watch a local run</u>
Every weekend, you can bet there will be a running race taking place. You can easily find a list online via a simple search. I'd encourage you to go along and watch one. Not only do you get to cheer on the participants and get a feel for the atmosphere, but you'll also get to see the wide range of ages that take part in these

races. Trust me, there are plenty of people in their 60s and over that have left me in their dust in races. I often see many in that age group finishing in the top 25. And don't think that these are all ex-pros that have been doing it their whole lives – the majority haven't.

This alone should help to quieten the inner voice that tells you you're too old to run.

<u>Find your fitness age</u>

By measuring your current fitness, you can get a very good idea of your biological fitness age. It used to be that you needed to visit a lab, jump on a treadmill, and pop on an oxygen mask to do this. Nowadays, it's much simpler. Most good fitness watches will give you a pretty accurate biological fitness age based on your VO2 Max. VO2 Max is something that lots of athletes get slightly obsessed with, but the purpose of this book is to keep things simple and jargon-free. But if you want to read more about it, a simple Wikipedia search will tell you everything you need to know[6].

If you can't afford to splash out on a fitness watch, then you can start to get a good idea of your current fitness age by timing yourself walking 1 mile as quickly (but as safely) as you currently can. The times below will give you an idea of your current biological age based on good times for that age group[7][8].

Men
Under 12m 30s = 20-29
Under 13m = 30-39
Under 13m 30s = 40-49
Under 14m = 50-59
Under 15m = 60-69
Under 16m = 70+

Women
Under 13m 30s = 20-29
Under 14m = 30-39
Under 15m = 40-49

Under 15m 30s = 50-59
Under 16m = 60-69
Under 18m 30s = 70+

Visualise your best

Find a quiet spot where you can relax and close your eyes (but obviously read this next bit first). Now think back to a time in your life where you felt happy with your physical self. Perhaps this was running around with friends when you were a child. Maybe it was a sport you enjoyed when younger, or it could simply be a point in your life where you felt in tune with your body. How did you feel at this moment? Try and recall the energy and excitement that you felt and how you were in sync with your physical side. If there are no moments that come to mind, instead imagine your ideal image of your fitter self; how do you look and feel?

Hold these mental images in your mind, and remember, you can realise these feelings and much more.

As we move forwards through this book, you can bring to mind these images and feelings as a visualisation of where you want to get your fitness to.

CHAPTER 2

The fitness barrier: "I'm too unfit to run"

"I've just seen this person running down the street; they looked so cool."

SAID NO ONE EVER.

The Barrier

If you haven't exercised in a while, the most challenging thing is actually getting started. Looking back to the time when I started running again, I felt quite intimidated on those first few weeks of running. I knew I was out of shape and that my fitness was very low. In my head, I imagined everyone was staring at my red-faced attempts at running.

I suspect that most of this was purely in my mind, but mental or not, it is daunting the first time that we re-enter the realm of fitness, and there are stats to back this up. In a OnePoll study, running outside was rated as the second most intimidating exercise, only just behind lifting weights in the gym[9].

Aside from the psychological challenges, being unfit is also going to present some physical barriers to getting started.

During that first run after a long absence, there's no hiding from what your body is telling you, and that can be a tough pill to swallow. And the more unfit you are, the harder it is. We can easily end up in a position where we feel like we are just too far gone even to exercise. In the same OnePoll study, 37% of people believed they were too unfit to start exercising.

It's very easy to listen to the negative voices in your head telling you, "You're just beyond hope." and "Why are you bothering? Just give up.". But these voices are what keep you stuck. It's at this point that you need to counter these thoughts with positive reminders about why you're doing this, bringing to mind the vision of your fitter, younger self.

A good parallel to how unfitness can prevent us from exercising is money management. Just like you can build up a debt of money, you can build up a debt of fitness. And the more in debt you get, the harder it is to get out. Conversely, people in this situation start to spend more, not less, because they think, "Well, I'm in debt anyway, what's one more meal out going to matter?". And just as when you're in debt, you look at your bank balance less, so it follows that when you're unfit, you look in the mirror less and avoid the scales.

In a word, you get blinkered.

I remember one of the first indications I had that I was starting to put on weight was that my shirts didn't fit properly. So, this means I hadn't noticed in the mirror that I'd gained weight. Instead, I had to be too large to get into my clothes for it to register. I just wasn't seeing the truth right in front of my eyes, and when I did, I wasn't sure how to get started.

Essentially, we can boil down these barriers into two factors: a fear of being judged and a lack of confidence in our ability. If we can address these issues, we can overcome two of the biggest obstacles to starting exercising.

The Truth

"I've just seen this guy running down the street; he looked so cool." – said no one ever. Let's face it, no one looks good running. Runners are usually dressed in clothing that would likely see you banned from most respectable establishments. We'll have sweat pouring off us and our faces will at best be wobbling about – or at worst be contorted into odd expressions.

And it's not just running; the gym is much the same. Some people might be under the illusion that they look amazing while working out, but they are in the same boat as the rest of us. What I'm trying to emphasise here is that we are all on a pretty level playing field when it comes to how we look when exercising. Generally, in life, we spend a lot of time worrying about what other people think about what we're doing when actually, most people are just thinking about themselves – or worrying about what you think of them.

Everyone who exercises would have started somewhere, and a lot of those people would have been on their own journey from unfitness to fitness. I've found that runners are some of the most humble, inclusive and friendly people I have ever met. Far from judging you, they are more likely to be giving you a wave of camaraderie.

Sure, you'll always get a few idiots who will shout things as you run past. Some of the words I've had hurled at me over the years have included pearls of wisdom like "Oi! Mate! The marathon was last week." and "Run faster baldy.". I can see how this might be off-putting and intimidating to new runners, but it happens very rarely. When it does, I feel sorry for these people. I know that deep down, they are likely jealous that I'm doing something positive with my life. Something they probably don't have the motivation to do themselves. If this happens to you, remember that you're doing this for yourself and your own wellbeing. You don't need to justify it to anyone else, so let the doubters eat your dust. I always have massive respect for people starting out on the path to fitness. Actually, I'm usually a bit envious of all those amazing feelings they are going to experience for the first time on their journey.

In the process of writing this book, I came across the incredible story of Roger Wright, who has transformed his life through running. Roger went from 318lbs to running 66 marathons in just over 11 years. I contacted Roger, and he was generous enough to share his achievements in his own words. Here's Roger's story:

"Back in 2006, my wife and I attended the wedding of our niece in Boston. I took quite a few pictures, always preferring to be behind the camera instead of in front of it. And because it was a wedding. I joined in the festivities and had my share of drinks.

The next day I was going through the pictures, renaming the files with the names of the people in the pictures, when I stumbled across a picture of my wife and some guy who I didn't recognize.

I asked my wife, "Who is that guy beside you?".

At first, she thought I was joking but quickly realized I was serious and reluctantly said three words that brought my world crashing down around me; "That is you.".

I was shocked. I suffer from Prosopagnosia (face blindness), but surely, she must somehow be mistaken. Looking at the picture and focusing on the tie I was wearing I realized and accepted that she was right. It was me. In order to try and save face (no pun intended), I immediately tried to regain my composure, brush it off and did my best to convince her that I was only joking around.

It seemed to work, but in retrospect, I now doubt that she actually bought it and felt bad for me. That is the kind of person she has always been.

I have always hated pictures of myself. I have been obese my entire life, moving into the 'hefty' category when I was around 10. There have been so many "That's it, damn it!" moments where my eyes were opened. I'd tell myself, "This time it will be different, and it will work!". I tried in earnest to lose weight, be it a new diet, joining a new health club, Weight Watchers – you get the idea.

Like a broken record, I would lose a few pounds and eventually, after a few days, start my fall off of the diet wagon and, at the same time, find excuses why I couldn't exercise that day.

By the end of the week, the plans that started out so optimistically had been completely derailed. I blamed everything other than myself for its failure, eventually moving on to a new approach to weight loss the following week or month.

This cycle continued over and over for approximately 25 years.

I'd convince the person staring back at me in the mirror (which happened less as I gained more weight) that I wasn't 'that' heavy. As far as pictures, I'd justify it by saying that it was just a bad picture thanks to *a poor angle, lighting or the person taking it.*

It's strange, but even though the scale said 318 and the pants I wore had a 54-inch waist, I would always come back to my belief that I was really only 20–30 pounds overweight. Although illogical and delusional, somehow, I could justify these thoughts. To a normal person, it doesn't really make sense, but speaking from my own experience, it did.

And that is why this picture from the wedding hurt me a little bit. No, it actually hurt me a lotta bit more.

It was around that time, when I was 45, that I decided to finally keep a promise I'd made to my wife that I'd go to see a doctor when I was 40. The doctor confirmed that I was as bad as I feared (actually worse), and she reluctantly suggested gastric bypass surgery, which I had read about and desperately wanted. To me, it promised an easy fix to a lifelong battle with my weight. Plus, unlike actually sticking to a diet and increasing my exercise, it took no discipline on my part other than attending a mandatory pre-surgery seminar and signing some papers.

Within two weeks, I happily found myself at a hospital in Boston listening to the mandatory 3-hour info session about the voluntary surgery. At the beginning, I received all of the positive news that I had anticipated and even more that I hadn't. But, as required, they also pointed out the few possible negatives of the surgery, such as 3% mortality, potential future internal issues and so on. I was surprised to find myself walking out and shaking my head. This was not the answer. The surgery would not be my savior.

It's a very long story, but after a series of events that happened in one week in May 2008 (I had just turned 47), and even though I hated running and had never really run a mile in my life, I decided to run the 2009 Boston Marathon, a race my father had run when I was seven years old. In the process, I could raise money for Cystic Fibrosis, a disease my niece suffers from. And I could lose some weight, hopefully around 50 pounds.

When I told my wife my plan, she looked at me with tears in her eyes and said, "I think it's important. If you do, I'll have a friend at every mile.". We hugged, and that sealed the commitment I'd made to her, as well as to my niece Julia.

I had just ten months. And every day of those ten months as I worked out and felt like giving up, I kept repeating the following mantra to myself; "If I fail, I have failed her. If I let her down, I have let us down.".

So, what happened? In ten months, I lost 125 pounds and went from running ten yards to running all 26.2 miles of the 2009 Boston Marathon – nonstop. My life changed forever.

A few days before I ran the race, I made a Cystic Fibrosis fundraising video soliciting donations that I sent to friends and family. A year and a half later, a friend asked if he could repost and rename the video, and I agreed. It ended up going viral with over 9 million views, and he called it (embarrassingly) 'The Most Inspiring Video You Will Ever Watch'.

The picture that started this story was taken 13 years ago. Today, I continue to run marathons and have just completed number 66 three weeks ago. Every time I cross the finish line, I give thanks for the chance I've had to finally change my life.

I often tell people that, before I lost my weight, if I happened to be in a room with 100 of my friends and asked each of them who would be the very last person that they thought could run a marathon, I would be that person. Of all of my friends that I have posed this question to, they have all agreed, without exception, that I WOULD have been their last pick. Until I started training for my first marathon at the age of 47, I had never run even 1 mile in my entire life. As much as I admired marathon runners, I despised running and never believed I could run 1 mile, let alone 26.2. I have now discovered that if you truly desire to accomplish an 'impossible' goal, it can be done if you give up excuses, believe in yourself and take the steps necessary to achieve that goal."

I'm sure you'll agree that Roger's story is truly inspirational.

This alone should help to give people who think they are too unfit to run the confidence they need to overcome their inhibitions and start running.

Runners are an eclectic mix of all shapes, sizes and abilities. By taking that first step, you will instantly become part of this worldwide community of like-minded people.

The Actions

There really is no reason to feel self-conscious before running, but I understand this is easier said than done. Following are some things you can do that will make it simpler to start and help overcome unfitness as a barrier to exercise.

Use the positive power of social

There is a whole community of runners online. Whether in real life or online, running is an inclusive sport where people of all levels come together to share stories, advice and encouragement. A quick google of any running-related questions will result in endless streams of conversations and blogs.

Some great spaces for new runners are online-only running communities like UKRunChat[10] and Lonely Goat Running Club,[11] of which I'm a member.

There are also some fun online running competitions open to all. For instance, The Vitality Running World Cup is an online-only running competition where anyone can run for their country and upload their miles using their fitness tracker or smartphone. They even let you create your own country running top so even us amateurs can run with our country flag emblazoned on our chests.

I would encourage you to join some of these communities and share any thoughts, fears and questions you have. Then even when training by yourself, this can help give you a sense of belonging to this huge global community of runners. As you progress on your own running journey, you can then share your stories and offer encouragement to others just starting out.

Run with friends

For me, running is an almost meditative pursuit. Personally, I enjoy the solitary nature of the sport and like setting my own pace and finding my own trail. Broadly, runners seem to fall into two camps, those who run alone and those who find their fuel running with friends. It probably depends on whether you are more introverted or more extroverted.

Running with friends, family, or colleagues is an excellent way to find the courage and motivation to get running. After all, it makes it much harder to hide under the duvet when you know you have your friend outside waiting for you.

If your friends think the thought of running is crazy, then why not join one of your local running clubs. Again, these will have runners of all abilities and will hold training sessions from beginners through to advanced level.

Remember, the hardest thing is getting started. Once you have a couple of runs under your belt, your body's natural endorphins will give you the feel-good-factor you need to keep going.

It's worth repeating here that if you haven't exercised in a long time – or ever – then it's essential you consult your doctor and have a general health check. This will enable you to plan your starting point and make sure you're not overdoing it to begin with.

CHAPTER 3

The illness barrier: "I'm too sick to run"

"I look like a rule breaker, but I'm not really; I just believe that nobody fully knows how the human body and brain work together, so I'm prepared to take a chance and look at something out of the ordinary."

AIS NORTH

The Barrier

I have to start this chapter by referring you to the medical disclaimer at the start of this book. I'm not medically trained, so it goes without saying that before you begin any exercise, especially post-illness, you should always consult your doctor to get the green light. This chapter aims to give inspiration and advice to those coming back from illness, but it's always vital to seek professional medical advice if you are new to running.

Illness is an inevitable part of life. We all get sick, and we have to accept that this will impact our training at some point. We're not talking about minor sniffles here; this section is about more serious illnesses and how we can get through them and return to running afterwards.

Any serious illness will mark a turning point in life. For those who don't exercise, it may be the wake-up call they need to start to transform their health for the better. For those that do, it may mean a frustrating break in activity followed by a gradual return to form.

The good news for those in the latter group is that all the hard work that they've put in earlier will not have gone to waste thanks to muscle memory. Muscle memory is a powerful aid to recovery, and something that anyone going through an illness-enforced break can take comfort from. The bodies of people that have previously trained to a decent level have been proven to bounce back much faster.

Studies have shown[12] that when you exercise, the neural pathways connecting the brain and your muscles get more entrenched so that when you return to running after a break, you'll be able to pick up more quickly than before.

Whatever your starting point following an illness, it's clear that it's going to present some significant physical and mental barriers to be overcome.

The Truth

I've read lots of humbling accounts about how people have overcome illness and returned to running. One that really stuck with me was that of Ais North, the septuagenarian ultra-runner we met in chapter 2.

Ais knows more than most about recovering from illness. She has had to deal with a heart attack, cancer, and back problems – yet still, she keeps running.

How does she find the resilience to do this? Ais was generous enough to offer to share her experiences in her own words.

"Back in 1997, when I was living in London and had two young children, I was diagnosed with breast cancer, DCIS, and I had surgery to remove my right breast and lymph nodes plus radiotherapy and chemotherapy. My family were devastated, and I needed to show I was ok. I was running a small business with quite a few employees and I knew that I had to remain the 'face' of the company at the very least. To cope mentally and physically, I started running along the Thames from Kew Bridge to Chiswick Bridge and back about 5k. I hadn't run for 20 years, but somehow, I knew instinctively that this would clear my head, help me cope with the radiotherapy and the chemo drugs and make sure that my family saw that I was recovering. Running is definitely in my DNA and it impacted me positively when I had cancer.

I only seem to get the big stuff; I rarely pick up bugs, never had flu and rarely succumb to feeling sick. Roll forward to 2017 and I've successfully completed the Fling Race, I've got some points towards the UTMB, and I'm feeling really positive about my running. That year, we holiday in Madeira, and I go off for a run alone up a big hill and feel great. Four days later when I'm home, I have a heart attack.

What? Me! No way. I am A-typical. I won't list why but you won't catch me eating cream cakes or putting sugar in my tea.

Enter the doctors, the nurses and all those folks that want you to get well but also believe you must stop running. "You have to face it, Ais, you may never run again.". Yeh right! The drugs and exercises they give you seem to assume that you're overweight and very unfit. Err No! I had an uphill battle to get them to understand that I could already lift a 20kg weight, that I ran almost daily – at least 35 miles a week – and that I didn't have a bad diet.

What they didn't help with, which I did get and had never had before, was depression. Whilst everyone else on the recovery programme was getting fitter and losing weight, I was becoming unfit and gaining weight. It was a bad experience and far worse than recovering from breast cancer. I did eventually find a specialist who looked after athletes that had heart attacks, mostly younger ones, and she said to go ahead and run a bit after she got my treadmill test results. They kept me on some of the drugs, saying they would help with heart repair, but I was off virtually all of them within a year. Just one more to check on, but the Covid-19 pandemic has slowed that down.

The heart attack impacted my running for the whole of 2018. Professionally, I changed course and worked full-time for an organisation out of the Manchester area, leaving little time for exercise. This meant that when I did return to running regularly in early 2019, I was almost back to square one. I'd lost my chance at the UTMB because I no longer had enough points.

But undeterred, off I went again with the aim of running a 50km race in the summer of 2019. In fact, I did two and managed a decent time for both, even improving in the second race, which was harder. I was back and on course to try for those points again when BAM, I was hit again. Turns out my life, not just my recent running, has taken its toll on my intervertebral discs. I've never had lower back pain in my life, but now my sciatic nerve decided to scream at me. I couldn't put my foot down, or even stand upright. The doctors told me; "You prob-

ably won't run again.", "You may need an injection to relieve the pain.", "You'll probably still be able to go for walks though.", "Dismissed!".

The mystery of my long-time painful glute was finally solved. Needless to say, I didn't believe that I would never run again, so I sought other advice and refused the painkilling injection and slowly began to recover through physio-strengthening exercises and a lot of online research. I'm not home and dry, and the furthest I have run since then is 20 miles. It's not completely comfortable, and I probably shouldn't push myself so much. I feel pain every day, and I keep working on the exercises. I have huge moments of self-doubt and a little fear that my nerve will 'scream' again. I can't run quite as fast and it's annoying, but it is improving. The UTMB seems very far away, but I won't ever give up. I'm determined to be better than I was in 2017, and I will work hard to get there. And despite what the medics said, I can run.

My short-term goal was to run 70 miles in October 2020; my 70th birthday was on the 7th. But then, in 2020, Covid hit and all the races were cancelled. However, I did manage an 80 km virtual trail race in the summer a couple of months before my 70th, so I'm very happy with that. My back still tweaks, as do my glutes, but I continue with the strength and flexibility exercises, and I am now researching the science of 'brain and pain'."

I'm sure you'll agree, Ais's courage and determination in the face of illness are incredibly motivating. It shows that if we are able to dig deep enough, we can find our way through illness and out the other side.

The Actions

With her own extensive experience of overcoming illness, I asked Ais to give her views on positive actions that people can take to overcome illness. Here's her advice:

<u>There's more than one route to getting better</u>
"The medical profession offers the standard advice through their

lens, don't ignore it, but search for other solutions if the one they give you causes you grief. I look like a rule breaker, but I'm not really; I just believe that nobody fully knows how the human body and brain work together, so I'm prepared to take a chance and look at something out of the ordinary."

Stop, breathe and reassess

"Taking a break in 2018, doing something different and reassessing what I wanted out of my running reaffirmed my desire and need to continue in the ultra-running field. If all else fails and your illness really does stop you from doing something that you love, it will hurt. Then you really do need to take a deep breath and look for another sport or hobby that thrills you as much. I know that I researched stand up paddleboarding and swimming as alternatives to running and would definitely consider them again if I did have to stop."

Don't over anticipate; simply participate

"Illnesses can knock your confidence and it's easy to think 'I shouldn't run in case I bring my illness back again', even when you are feeling better. Gauge how you feel and if you're feeling up to it, get out there. Don't let overthinking or catastrophising about what could happen get in the way of what you want to do. You don't have to smash any world records, but simply showing up could help kickstart your journey back to health."

CHAPTER 4

The fear barrier: "I'm too anxious to run"

"It's understandable how people end up feeling isolated with their mental health problems. It can feel like wading through a thick soup to do anything when your mind is sapping strength from your body."

CLINT LOVELL

The Barrier

As I mentioned in the introduction, I have a long experience of dealing with anxiety. Why it started, I still really have no clear idea. Nothing that I've been able to pinpoint is an obvious cause, and this is often the case for those with anxiety.

I first started getting panic attacks at the age of 16. At this time, I had no idea what they were, which only added fuel to the fear. One moment I'd be fine; the next, I would be shaking, ashen-faced, and sometimes vomiting. And the worst bit was, I'd never know when it would strike. This led to me being fearful of leaving the house in case I had an anxiety attack.

By the time I got to my early 20s, and while studying at university, I was struggling daily. I had become a master at hiding my anxiety attacks from everyone but myself, which only added to the burden. At my lowest, depression set in. I couldn't sleep properly, I couldn't eat, and every day was a constant cycle of panic attacks. I'd had enough, and I was even starting to think that I wouldn't be able to go on living like this for much longer.

At this point, I reached out to my parents and explained everything I'd been experiencing. Luckily, they were able to put me in touch with a family friend who was a professional psychologist. Once I understood what I was experiencing and that I wasn't losing my mind, I was able to gradually start to improve my mental health.

The challenge for anyone dealing with mental health problems is that we often become more introverted, which in turn makes us more isolated. In my case, I was fearful of even leaving my house, let alone getting outside and exercising. When fear, anxiety and depression take over, our world's shrink and the walls close in. Anxiety steals our adventurous spirit and depression crushes our motivation.

We become trapped in our heads, and our thoughts become our prison.

The Truth

It's understandable how people end up feeling isolated with their mental health problems. It can feel like wading through a thick soup to do anything when your mind is sapping strength from your body, so it's no wonder people stay stuck. But it doesn't have to be inevitable.

For myself, once I understood what was happening, I became determined not to be hemmed in by my anxiety. I started to realise that if I was feeling fear all the time anyway, I may as well try and do the things I wanted to do.

The curious thing with anxiety is that once you willingly put yourself in the situations you fear and confront the worst-case scenario, you actually start to fear those situations less. Slowly but surely, your world begins to get bigger again. Using this coping strategy of constantly pushing my boundaries and getting outside my comfort zone, I have chased my anxiety to the edges of my life and expanded my world to the point where I can lead a life where anxiety is in the background, not centre stage.

Running has been a huge help to me in managing my anxiety. Once I started to venture out again following the worst of my anxiety, I would often go walking alone for hours and hours. Just getting fresh air and raising my heart rate helped me to walk away some of the nervous energy. Slowly these walks became runs and I started to experience the benefit of the endorphins flooding my body. But most of all, I was taking back control of my situation; I was chasing the anxiety away. For the first time in years, I felt that I was back in the driving seat.

It's understandable when we are trapped by anxiety and depression that we start to feel like we are no longer in control of our lives. We become ruled by our negative thoughts. In contrast, when we start to take positive action, we immediately begin to feel more in control of our lives. Both negativity and positivity can be a fuel, but when we flip to a positive perspective, we have suddenly reversed the energy system of the body.

If you are struggling with your own mental health challenges, I would urge you to try running. As I said at the beginning, it won't cure you, but it will make you feel more in control and give your brain a positivity boost. You'll be doing something amazing for your mind and your body.

I would like to say that since my mental turnaround, it has been a fairytale and that I literally ran into the sunset happily ever after, but life isn't ever that simple. There have been many mental peaks and troughs in the 20 years since my university days, and there were periods in my late 20s and early 30s where I forgot the benefits that running could have on my mental health.

But when I came back to running in my early 30s after a physical slump, I once again discovered the powerful positive effects it would have on both my mental and physical health. Since this point, and with ten plus years of running several times a week, my physical body has been transformed, but most importantly, I know that whatever life throws at me, running will always help keep my mental outlook more positive and more balanced.

The Actions

Make your world bigger, not smaller
This is the simplest but also the hardest thing to do. As I have spoken about in this chapter, anxiety often closes in the walls around us as we attempt to avoid all fear-inducing situations. In life, this is never going to be possible. Personally, I like to take the approach of doing one thing that scares me every day. These

don't have to be big things; they can be small things too and will be very specific depending on your particular fears. Maybe it's going to the shops, meeting new people or leading a presentation at work – whatever it is, set the challenge and then keep pushing those boundaries further out. The space you create will also create more calm.

Talk to people

Speak to friends, but also consider speaking to mental health professionals. It's something that I've always found massively helpful. Mental health issues can naturally make us very introspective when often we need to share our problems and challenges with others. Sometimes just airing your fears can make you feel much better. Talking while getting active can also be great, so why not try running with friends and having a chat along the way? Sometimes the outdoors can give your thoughts the room that they need.

Get active

Obviously, with this being a running book, I'm going to suggest getting out there for a run. But any exercise can be beneficial to an anxious mind. If you're not ready to run just yet, simply get out there and fill your lungs with fresh air. I guarantee that you'll feel better. If you can get active in nature, even better. There's something incredibly restorative about being close to the natural world and away from the noise and distractions of our busy modern lives. I love running in the woods or near water in the mornings. I find this really charges my mental batteries and sets me up for the day.

CHAPTER 5

The time barrier: "I'm too busy to run"

"Sometimes I feel guilty for running. Like I'm being selfish for taking time for me. But I try to remind myself that I'm setting an example for my daughter to be healthy by staying active – even when I'm busy."

DELORES DURKO

The Barrier

You've dropped your partner or kids off, commuted to work, had a crazy day in the office with back-to-back meetings, munched through a desk lunch, got held up at the office by that 5.24pm curveball, got delayed on the way home, grabbed dinner ingredients on the fly, fed the household, and now you might just get a minute to yourself before hitting repeat tomorrow.

Fancy a run anyone?

This is the problem that many of us experience in everyday life. Busyness is an affliction of modern life that we all succumb to at one point or another. So, is it any surprise that we don't feel like we have the time to exercise? Not really.

Busyness is a trap that we can all easily fall into – and once in, it's tough to find a way out. So, let's start by understanding how we end up caught.

The dream was a technology-enhanced utopia where we could all enjoy more leisure time and less work time. The reality is that we are busier than ever. Far from freeing us, technology actually keeps us plugged in at all times and all places. Now, even on holiday, your office can contact you and expect an immediate response.

Many factors increase our busyness, such as living further from work, working longer hours - as well as the myriad of digital distractions.

Our time is at a premium, and busyness has become our currency.

In her book, Overwhelmed[13], Brigid Schulte talks about how much value we put on being busy. And it's true. How often when asked how we are by a friend do we reply; "I've been really busy.".

We are wearing our busyness as a medal of honour. It's almost a way of proving our social worth and justifying our importance. But how much of that time is being used productively and effectively?

In the next section, we are going to see how we can escape busyness and find the time and energy for fitness.

The Truth

It's true that our personal lives are busier than ever, and that work is encroaching more and more into our leisure time, but how much of that time is being utilised effectively?

Not much according to Timothy Ferriss, author of the 4-hour work week[14]. He has adopted Vilfredo Pareto's 80/20 principle, a useful tool for gauging how efficiently we are actually using our time. This principle can be applied in many ways, but in terms of time management, it's used to illustrate that just 20% of our time creates 80% of the results. This means 80% of our time is probably being spent doing things that don't matter that much or don't bring that much value to our lives.

This may sound farfetched, but I bet for most of us, if we're really honest, it's not untrue. One study[15] found that people only had 2 hours and 48 minutes of productive time each day.

If we add up the hours that we spend looking at dogs skateboarding on Youtube, watching Netflix, or lost in a forest of emails, we can all probably see how we can carve out some more time in our days for exercise. But it's not easy. The busier we become, the more blinkered we get to everything else around us. There's even a term for this, 'Tunnelling'[16]. This is used to describe when our busy brains effectively shut out other external input to lower our mental bandwidth. The problem is it also lowers our IQ by as much as 13 points.

So, we can say without exaggeration that the busier we become, the stupider we get, and the worse our decision-making will be.

I'm not underestimating the challenge here. I know from my own experiences as a busy parent, how hard it can be to find more time. I've always been especially in awe of busy mums who manage to fit running and exercise into their crammed schedules. I wanted to hear first-hand how these amazing mums manage this juggling act, so I reached out on social media. Delores Durko, a busy North American mother, was happy to share her story in her own words.

"I've been a runner off and on since high school. I was usually pretty good about staying active and eating somewhat healthily but I would get away from it occasionally, mostly because my now ex-husband had very poor habits, overeating unhealthy foods and spending a lot of time plopped in front of the TV. I was in pretty decent shape when I had our daughter at the age of 34. But I gained quite a bit of weight throughout and after the pregnancy. I'm nearly 5'10" but weighed 226 pounds. I was overweight, unhealthy and miserable. I would blame my baby weight, but my daughter had just turned 4, so that excuse was no longer feasible.

I remember distinctly taking a load of laundry upstairs and being completely winded. I thought to myself, 'this isn't right. I shouldn't have this much trouble going up a flight of stairs.' I decided right then that I was going to do something about it. I started Weight Watchers online and began walking on our treadmill every day. The weight started to come off. I had more energy and felt better than I had in years. So, I kept going. When I hit a plateau, I would re-evaluate. I started running on the treadmill. Then, a friend invited me to run a 5k race. I had never run outside and loved it. I was hooked. I vowed to myself that I would continue to run and lead a healthy lifestyle no matter what was going on in my life.

As a parent, I do have to be a bit creative with the timing of my runs, such as running at a different time than I prefer – I like early morning runs best. Ultimately, people make time for the things that they want to do. I love running. It's part of who I am, and it's important to me. Even if it means getting up at 5am to squeeze in a run before work and dropping my daughter off at school, I will make every effort to do so. There are mornings where I want to stay in bed and scrap my run, but I remind myself how I will feel if I don't.

Sometimes I feel guilty for running. Like I'm being selfish for taking time for me. But I try to remind myself that I'm setting an example for my daughter to be healthy by staying active – even when I'm busy. I also know that I need running for my mental well-being. I have anxiety disorder and running is my medicine. It helps clear my head.

Pushing through tiredness is something I've been battling more lately. Between job stress, getting chores done, errands and hormone fluctuations from perimenopause, it has been a struggle. My doctor told me to keep running. Nothing will help me more with stress, anxiety, and my peri-menopausal symptoms than staying active. I have noticed in days that I don't do any kind of activity, I'm more likely to wear out before the end of my day. I sometimes get fatigued because of hormones, but I just try to power through knowing that I'm doing what's best for my body. I just have to give my brain a pep talk.

To keep motivated to run, I try to remind myself how I will feel if I don't run. All runners struggle with motivation at some point. I have to get out early in the day – if I wait too long, I might talk myself out of it. I always try to remember that I never regret a run, even if it's a short run, it is better than nothing. You either make time or make excuses."

Reading Delores' account shows how running can help us tap into energy reserves and cope with our packed schedules. And as we've heard, if the average person is only using 20% of their time effectively, there must be more time available for fitness.

Next, in the actions section, we'll check out some practical ways that we can find the time to exercise.

The Actions

Complete your own time audit

One of the best ways to find extra time in your schedule for exercise is to make a diary of all the activities you do in your day – and I mean ALL the activities, however insignificant they may seem. We're trying to find the white space between the important tasks, so it's really important to be honest. Do this over a few days so you can get a rounded picture and start to see patterns in the activities.

Once you've got your list, go through it and mark each activity as either high value or low value. Remember that high-value things can be leisure activities like reading a novel – not just hyper-productive work tasks. Chances are, you'll be able to quickly identify tasks you can eliminate or certainly reduce. Maybe you're spending an hour each day grazing online news sites, filing unimportant emails, or sat in unproductive meetings.

The goal here is to try and free up 45 mins to 1 hour a day that we can use to exercise. That's all we're looking for, so it should be very achievable.

If you're still struggling to find those extra minutes, you could try getting up a little earlier in the morning. I've moved my wake-up time forward by about 45 minutes, and now I'm a big fan of running first thing. I'll often hit the trails before 7am with my exercise done before most people have even sipped their first cup of coffee. These have been some of my favourite runs where I've seen the sunrise and enjoyed the silent beauty of undisturbed nature.

Schedule exercise

Another tactic if you have a back-to-back working day is to schedule in your exercise time like a meeting. I book in lunch-time runs and gym sessions in my work calendar so everyone can see this. It helps prevent you from having to justify last minute that you're off to the gym. And don't cancel it unless it's an absolute emergency – and let's face it, unless the office is on fire, what is? Prioritise your exercise time like you would an important meeting. If your boss and colleagues still need convincing, just say you have a personal trainer session paid for and you'll lose your money if you don't go – this usually does the trick.

Exercise will make you more productive, not less productive. It will help snap you out of 'Tunnelling' mode so that when you do get back to what you were doing, you'll be more productive, and as we've learnt, about 13 points of IQ more intelligent.

There can be a tendency for us, especially those with partners and children, to feel that devoting time to exercise is a selfish pursuit. If you feel like this, remind yourself that by investing time in your health, you'll be more energised and more present in the quality moments that you do spend with your family. By winding back your biological age, you'll also be giving yourself a better chance of being around for your family for longer too.

These suggestions are just the start. In Chapter 7, we'll be looking at even more methods you can deploy to make running a simple and sustainable part of your routine.

CHAPTER 6

The fatigue barrier: "I'm too tired to run"

"I've learnt that every small step in the right direction takes me further from my worst days."

MARLENE LOWE

The Barrier

The strange thing was that even though I was doing less exercise than ever before, I felt more tired. But it's one of life's ironies that the less we do, the less we want to do.

I remember coming home from work worn out and then waking up at the weekend still feeling tired. It seemed like I was caught in a never-ending cycle of tiredness.

I began to convince myself that maybe it was just the start of getting older - I know, at thirty! The reality was that I was stuck in the tiredness trap.

When we break it down, there are two types of tiredness - physical and mental. At times, it can be quite hard to distinguish between the two.

I'm sure you'll be familiar with that feeling at the end of a long day in the office when you just feel exhausted. You may have sat in your comfy chair for nearly 8 hours straight, but you still feel pooped. This, unsurprisingly, is mental tiredness, and it often stops us from exercising by convincing us that we are too worn out.

But is this all just in our heads? Well, actually, no.

There is evidence to suggest that this mental fatigue does affect physical performance. In his book Endure[17], Alex Hutchinson recounts experiments with peak condition athletes where they have to complete a series of demanding mental tasks before hitting their exercise bikes. On average, the athletes gave up 15% sooner when mentally tired compared with their mentally refreshed selves.

It's probably fair to say that if it's having this effect on professional athletes, it's also going to play a part for us more average types, making it more difficult to get out the door and exercise at our most optimal

Let's not underestimate how physically tiring life can be too. Doing the household chores, rushing up the escalators, carrying the shopping home; all these things are still types of exercise and can add up throughout the day to create an accumulated feeling of tiredness.

The Truth

With the physical and mental tiredness that we build up in our days, it's easy to convince ourselves that we are too tired to go for that run. But if we're honest, are the majority of us really that tired?

To prove what's possible, I wanted to speak to people who have overcome extreme exhaustion to achieve their running goals. One story that grabbed my attention while researching this book was that of Marlene Lowe. She suffers from Myalgic Encephalomyelitis/Chronic Fatigue Syndrome (M.E./CFS) but still managed to summon the strength to run a 5km race. Here's her story.

"In February of 2017, I wrote an article about running for M.E./ CFS. The article was published on the blog 'The Mighty'[18] and was filled with positive affirmations and a head-strong resilience to make sure I got back to 'who I used to be'. I shared my journey into being diagnosed with M.E./CFS and the impact it had on my life – but that I had decided to 'beat it into submission'. I had lived with the diagnoses of M.E./CFS for almost four years by then, and changes to my working environment, plus having a fantastic doctor that was willing to try new medication, had me overcoming the worst of the everyday fatigue. I could hold down a job again, start seeing my friends, and read my books. Most of the worst of my symptoms had gone, and so running the BUPA 5 km for Action for M.E. was my way of showing that we can overcome disease.

Unfortunately, that was the last time I managed to turn to running. After the race, I hit a wall again and I stopped exercising. It was frustrating to have achieved something so pivotal in my recovery, only to have to go through another setback.

In hindsight, I can see now why this happened. It wasn't because of the run itself, and it wasn't because of work; it was because I had chosen to treat only one aspect of my life and decided that THAT meant I was getting better. When in reality, there were a lot of stressors in my life that were left unattended and untreated.

So today, I'd like to share another story with you. It has now been seven years since I was diagnosed with M.E./CFS. At my lowest, I found it hard to speak, count, work, see friends, and function the way I always had before. I was bed-bound during weekends and reliant on my then partner and my parents to survive. I will always and forever be thankful for the support I have had throughout my journey. Far too often you hear stories of people that are ridiculed or taunted, people that are not believed. Part of my recovery has been thanks to having people around me that took this disease seriously and did not shy away from the difficulties of having an invisible illness.

On the days where I felt 'normal' again, I was euphoric and wanted to do everything I loved on one single day – because who knew if this day would come back? Even on those good days though, there was something that was never really quite right, and the best thing I ever did was acknowledge this.

I said to myself: if something isn't quite right, I need to know why. And so began a three-year journey into finding out what worked for me and what didn't. I learnt to set boundaries for myself; I learnt to say no. Being a people pleaser, learning to say NO was one of the biggest hurdles I ever faced. I started looking at my relationships and the activities I did regularly and noticed which left me drained and which left me invigorated.

Once I had identified an 'energy vampire', I simply minimised my *exposure – or got rid of it entirely. Meditation became part of my week. These moments of calm helped give me energy to continue the day but also gave me insight into what else I needed to work on in life. In January of 2020 however, I had another relapse. This relapse saved my life. Depression and anxiety hit me like another sledgehammer and each week got worse than the last. One day, in the middle of February, I sat in my car and had a full meltdown. My mother, the voice of reason, told me I had to look for help. This is something I couldn't fix by myself; I needed to learn to ask for help. This piece of advice has transformed and saved my life.*

That very day I called the doctor. I got help through the NHS with medication for my anxiety and appointments to speak to someone. Three days after I started taking the medication, I started walking. Oh, the freedom! To be able to walk outside and feel calm again - this was the making of dreams. A week before COVID-19 hit the U.K. I decided to start speaking with a therapist. Taking medication has never been something I enjoy doing, but with the new mental clarity, I realised I had issues that needed to be resolved. Not least my journey through M.E./CFS!

Weekly appointments with a therapist meant I could stop taking my medication. Daily walks had me learning to breathe again, my own form of meditation and a chance to daydream. Each week I managed to walk a little bit further, push my body a little bit more. Thanks to COVID-19, I was forced to look at my life and take a moment to just be 'me'. That day in February, and lockdown, has quite literally saved my life. I sit here now, writing this, knowing that I no longer want to be 'the old me'. I just want to be a better version of myself. I have learnt to be thankful for my M.E./CFS – it has taught me to spend my time doing the things that bring me joy and spend time with the people that bring value to my life. It has taught me that the small achievements can add up to a great big adventure.

I've learnt that every small step in the right direction takes me further from my worst days. But that I have survived 100% of my worst days. I sit here now, proud, because yesterday I ran 5 km again. I cried.

I am not who I used to be, and I am working on being better. And that 5 km run would never have happened if I hadn't taken those first steps for a small walk."

I think we can all be moved by Marlene's account. It really does show what it is possible to do, even in the face of crushing fatigue. And with the Covid-19 pandemic causing long-term fatigue and post-viral symptoms in vast numbers of people, this battle with extreme exhaustion is something that is going to be even more prevalent.

Exercise isn't always the answer, and it isn't always advisable or achievable for some people. But what Marlene's story does show us is how it's possible to tap into the hidden energy reserves we have in our bodies if we are determined. We just need to learn how to access and activate them.

The Actions

Evaluate your tiredness

I'll let you into a secret. Running won't eliminate feelings of tiredness from your life. What it will do is boost your energy levels and release helpful endorphins that will in turn create a more virtuous circle.

However, our minds are very good at playing tricks on us. There'll be days when your mind will convince you that "I'm too tired to exercise.", or that "Maybe I'm going down with something." only for you to find that you lace up your trainers and hit the road to return buzzing and feeling great. This has happened to me countless times.

To try to counter this, I try to separate real exhaustion from the mind-manufactured variety.

So, if you're feeling tired, ask yourself, "Is this mental or physical?" if it's mental, and there's no good reason not to, get out there and get running. As we learnt earlier, mental fatigue may make the workout harder, and in extreme cases, less productive, but it shouldn't stop you. Chances are, you'll also feel much better and more positive after the run from the endorphin release.

If, on the other hand, the tiredness is physical, then ask yourself, "Am I ill, or just tired?". If simply tired, then you already know what to do! If you're ill with a chesty cough, sore throat, or swollen glands, then rest is definitely best. In a pre-Covid world, many runners used the above-the-neck rule where if your symptoms were above the neck, such as a blocked nose, you still run. Whereas if they are below the neck, as with a chest infection, you stay home. Post-Covid, it only seems responsible that if we have any symptoms of illness, then we should all act on the side of caution and rest up until better.

It's really all about using our common sense. We're not trying to run ourselves into the ground, figuratively or literally. This is about helping to make an honest assessment of your tiredness so that you don't fall into the trap of always feeling too tired to exercise. As Ais North stated earlier in the book, running tired is ok; running when exhausted isn't.

PART 2 – TRAINING YOUR BODY

CHAPTER 7

Creating a sustainable plan

Now we've been through the common barriers to running and ways to overcome them, hopefully, you'll now be eager to get running and putting theory into practice. But before we begin, it's essential to ensure that we're building an exercise plan that's sustainable. It's easy to get fired up about something at the beginning when your motivation and willpower are high, but, as we know, willpower is finite. So, how do we keep things going once that initial excitement has passed?

Really, it's quite simple; we have to create a routine that fits into our busy lives. We've already discovered how busyness and tiredness are traps we can easily fall into, and if we're not careful, these will quickly take over and smother our carefully made exercise plans.

Hopefully, by following the actions in Chapter 5, you've been able to see areas of your life where you can carve out chunks of time for running. Now we need to protect that time.

Following, are my seven rules that you can use to help create a lasting exercise plan. I'm calling them rules and not tips because you do need to be strict with them to ensure that things don't slip. This isn't about being rigid and unbending; it's about creating a flexible structure that can move and adapt with your life.

1. Get Out There Whatever The Weather

Let's be honest, if we waited for the perfect weather condi-tions before we went running outside, we'd rarely ever do it.

Unless you're lucky enough to live in Los Angeles, you're likely to experience changeable weather. And thanks to its island climate, it doesn't get more unpredictable than where I live in the UK. I often hear friends and colleagues say variations of "I was going to go running, but it was too wet.". Too wet, too cold, too snowy, too icy, too hot – the list can be endless, and it's all too easy to let the weather be our excuse. But an excuse is exactly what it is.

Over the years, I've run in snowstorms, heatwaves, torrential rain, thunder, and ice – you name it, I'll be out there in it. I can say with my hand on my heart that some of these have been the most exhilarating runs I have ever done.

What can be better than leaving a trail of fresh trainer prints in the snow?

The best approach is to make sure you have the running gear to suit every occasion. Invest in some warm leggings and a top. If you're running on icy ground, switch to a trail shoe that offers more grip. Above all, plan ahead by checking the weather forecast and get that kit ready the night before, so you're ready to run.

If it is honestly too bad to get outside, you can always substi-tute the run for a treadmill session or a burst on the exercise bike. Just don't let it interrupt your exercise plans.

2. Make Running Part Of Your Commute

Working in a city, I have to commute. It's easy to see your commute as an endless drain on time and energy when really it can be an ideal opportunity to fit some exercise into your day.

If you're in the lucky few people who live relatively close to their work, why not start running one way – or even better both ways – to the office? This is a fantastic way to start and end each day and will have you zipping into your office full of life while your colleagues are still bleary-eyed and chugging down a big coffee. If, on the other hand, you have to get a train to work, why not start running to your station and then from your station to work? This is what I do, and it allows me to sneak in a good 8 miles a day around my workday. You can also start getting off the train earlier if you want to increase that weekly mileage. When training for longer runs, I'll get off the train 15 miles from home and finish the journey on foot. This is a brilliant way of squidging in your long run without losing hardly any time from your week.

Maybe you have to drive to work. But again, this shouldn't be a barrier. Why not park your car further from work and run the last bit? You'll be racking up the miles before you know it in a way that will have a really minimal time impact on your day.

One other barrier to running to work that I hear a lot is "But, we don't have showers!". Don't let this stop you. Yes, a shower is great, but a wet wipe shower is just as good. Trust me, you won't smell.

If you're required to be formally dressed for work, make sure you have smart shoes that you can leave at the office. You'll also need to think ahead a bit and make sure you take in a set of work clothes on one of your non-running days.

Whatever the obstacles are that come up in your mind, they are all solvable and will quickly become a regular and easy part of your routine.

3. Have A Break, Have A Run

Lunchtime runs are the best. Not only do they ensure that you get some quality exercise during what's normally dead time, but they will also re-energise you for the afternoon.

I try and do at least one lunch run a week. I find that they really help to clear my head from the morning and make me extra productive in the afternoon.

You might need to plan a little bit more around these runs. If you think you'll get hungry, make sure you have a mid-morning snack planned. And don't cancel your run because you're too busy. Of course, you need to be flexible and move it around where necessary but as I mentioned earlier, make sure that you schedule it in your work diary so everyone can see it. Then stick to it.

These days, most sensible workplaces are investing huge amounts in employee well-being, so it's unlikely you'll have to explain the benefits too much. If you do, it's quite simple; healthy, happy employees are super-productive employees.

4. Take Your Trainers On Holiday

Holidays, time for a rest, right? Nope! Sure, we all want to kick back a bit on our holidays and enjoy a few days lounging around, but I'd strongly recommend taking your trainers on holiday.

Running in foreign and exotic locations can be an absolutely fantastic way of seeing a place. I love to run on holiday, it makes you feel really connected to the place that you are visiting, and you'll experience so much more while on foot.

It's enabled me to find great little beaches, excellent restaurants, and hidden away corners of islands. If you think it might be too hot, too cold, and so on, then you already know the answers to those thoughts.

5. See The Sunrise And The Sunsets

Running early and running late are great ways of making your exercise more sustainable. If you're running early, make sure you have everything ready the night before. This is really important as you want to remove any potential hurdles to getting your trainers on. It's hard enough waving goodbye to your duvet without then having to rummage through your drawers half asleep to find everything. The trick is to make it so simple that you can run on autopilot and be out the door before your mind has even had time to object.

If you're more of a night owl, then why not dispense with some of that dead time in the evenings that are likely spent watching TV or surfing social and instead go for a run? You'll work off lots of the nervous energy from the day and be ready to wind down properly before you hit your bed.

The general wisdom is that you shouldn't exercise too late and certainly not just before bed, as this can leave your body overstimulated on all the endorphins and could actually make it harder for you to get to sleep.

6. Track Your Progress, Share Your Success

Some runners love fitness trackers, and others don't. It's fair to say that a few people do get a bit too obsessive about the stats, endlessly pouring over them and then getting distressed by even minor changes to their performance. Used in the right way, though, fitness trackers are a brilliant way to stay motivated. It enables you to see when progress is being made and to set and achieve your goals.

Using platforms like Strava, Fitbit, or Garmin Connect, to name a few, you can build up your own support groups of runners and get encouragement from your friends and family. These also allow you to see where you stack up in terms of times with your peers and people running the same routes – depending on how serious you want to get. As mentioned earlier, there are many online-only races, such as The Vitality Running World Cup, where you can compete in your own time and then upload your results to take part.

All of these things will definitely help add to your motivation to keep training and improve your fitness.

7. Create Milestone Moments

Whether it's setting your own goals, or entering races with specific targets in mind, putting a few milestones throughout your year will help you get a real sense of achievement. I usually enter a race or event roughly every eight weeks throughout the year. I find this helps ensure that I always have a race to focus my training on, but it also helps me measure my performance and, hopefully, get satisfaction from the results. The great thing about running is that, with the exception of the London Marathon, the events are relatively cheap to take part in. That means you can book in your runs for the year without it being a disaster if you're ill. And I'll always accept that one run a year will most likely be scuppered by illness. Some of the bigger runs and marathons will offer insurance for precisely this purpose so you can get your money back or get a free entry for the following year. It's good to mix things up a bit too. Rather than just doing lots of 5ks over a year, try experimenting with some obstacle runs like Tough Mudder or maybe some hill running events. This will help to keep things varied and also test your body in new ways.

If you apply these seven rules, I can guarantee that you will make exercise a more sustainable part of your life. You'll start to fit running into your schedule in a way that takes minimal effort and maximises downtime that wasn't being used that effectively before.

If, at any point, your training starts to feel like a chore or your motivation has hit a brick wall, stop and think why. Revisit these seven rules again as well as the actions from the chapters on busyness and tiredness and try and highlight what's changed and where you need to refocus.

These things take a little bit of time to become part of your day-to-day too. To begin with, it's going to feel different but keep going. Every week of training that you do, it will become more ingrained in your everyday life.

CHAPTER 8

Beginning your training

I certainly don't profess to be the world's best runner, but I hope to bring a fresh perspective to training. When I was initially researching running plans online, I found a lot of them were written by ex-professional athletes. On one level, this is great as they have achieved things others never can, but it also means that they have a very different perspective to the average person who is building from nothing. I found many to be hard to understand and overly filled with jargon.

My aim here is to create simple plans that are built from the perspective of people who are doing this for the first time. That's why I've tried to keep the terminology light and the instructions clear.

As well as my personal experience in building my fitness, I'm also drawing on the knowledge from my Level 2 Fitness Instructor qualification and my Level 3 Personal Trainer course. So, although I'm not an ex-pro athlete or leading running coach, I am writing this from a point of qualified understanding of the physical body.

Depending on natural and current fitness levels, everyone is going to have their own starting points. Maybe you're already pretty fit, and you're ready to dive straight into your 10k training. Or, perhaps this is the first time you've ever properly considered running. Whatever your level, there's a starting point that will be right for you.

As I've already stressed, if this is your first time exercising in a while, or ever, it's important that you speak to your doctor and get a clean bill of health before beginning. Once you have that, you're good to go.

The rest of this chapter outlines plans for all different levels and abilities. The first plan is for those with little, if any, experience of running. This will take you from nothing up to 5k a week.

The next plan is aimed at getting you ready to run your first 10k. This will build on the first plan and start to increase distance and frequency of training.

Plan three is for those that can comfortably run a 10k race and are ready to start pushing their limits and training for their first half marathon.

Finally, I have included some advanced plans for those looking to realise new targets and achieve a sub-40-minute 10k time and a sub-90-minute half marathon time. We'll go into more detail as to why these times are important benchmarks in those sections.

Starting Your Journey – The 5 Weeks To 5K Plan

Most of this book's focus has been about removing the barriers and life distractions that stop us from starting to run. Hopefully, you're now ready and excited to start your new running adventure. Although getting started is the most difficult step, it's also the most rewarding. When you are taking your fitness levels from pretty much nothing, you're going to start to notice some giant leaps in improvements. These won't be all at once from day one, but incremental improvements will accumulate and build momentum like a juggernaut running down a hill.

In this section, I've set out an achievable plan that will take you from running your first steps right up to a 5k race. If you have never run before, or not run in a long while, 5k can seem like a big target to reach, but this distance is very achievable for everyone that's willing to put the training in.

The plan covers 5 weeks. The reason being that 5 weeks will give you time to build up your stamina and let your body adjust to the new things you'll be asking of it. It will also be a reasonable amount of time for you to establish a new, healthy routine that's going to be sustainable.

At the end of this section, there is a diagram that gives an overview of the plan so you can see it all together in one place. Next, we'll break down each week and detail what the activities are and why each one is important.

Week 1
For this week, and some of the initial weeks of training, there's a mix of walking and running. This is to allow you to build up your fitness gradually and make sure that the body has time to adapt to running. It takes time for your muscle groups to adapt and strengthen to the movements of running, and this will enable you to do this in a way that won't shock the body. Think of it as running in the engine on a new car.

Mon: 2-minute walk, 2-minute run. Repeat 5 times.
Tues: Rest.
Weds: 2-minute walk, 2-minute run. Repeat 5 times.
Thurs: Rest.
Fri: Rest.
Sat: 2-minute walk, 2-minute run. Repeat 5 times.
Sun: Rest.

Week 2
This week, you'll be building your stamina by extending the running times further. By the end of the week, you'll be aiming to run 16 minutes in 4 intervals.

Mon: 3-minute walk, 3-minute run. Repeat 4 times.

Tues: Rest.
Weds: 3-minute walk, 3-minute run. Repeat 4 times.
Thurs: Rest.
Fri: Rest.
Sat: 4-minute walk, 4-minute run. Repeat 4 times.
Sun: Rest.

Week 3

Now your focus is on beginning to run for longer with shorter walking intervals. This will start to build up your aerobic capacity. By the end of the week, you should be running 24 minutes in 3 intervals.

Mon: 3-minute walk, 6-minute run. Repeat 3 times.
Tues: Rest.
Weds: 3-minute walk, 6-minute run. Repeat 3 times.
Thurs: Rest.
Fri: Rest.
Sat: 2-minute walk, 8-minute run. Repeat 3 times.
Sun: Rest.

Week 4

This week you'll be continuing to build up your endurance and running longer without stopping. By the end of the week, you'll be able to run 15 minutes without stopping.

Mon: 10-minute run, 1-minute walk. Repeat 3 times.
Tues: Rest.
Weds: 10-minute run, 1-minute walk. Repeat 3 times.
Thurs: Rest.
Fri: Rest.
Sat: 12-minute run, 3-minute walk. Repeat 2 times.
Sun: 15-minute run.

Week 5

Great work on making it to week 5. Now, it's time for race week, where you can put all that practice into your first race performance. Remember, this is about completing the race, not setting new records. You should aim to start at a comfortable pace and build up speed as you move through each kilometre. In the excitement of the race, it's very easy to start too fast. This will always lead to a lag at the end of the race. You should target a pace that's slightly faster than your training runs.

Mon: 15-minute run, 1-minute walk. Repeat 2 times.
Tues: Rest.
Weds: 10-minute run, 1-minute walk. Repeat 3 times.
Thurs: Rest.
Fri: 10-minute run, 1-minute walk. Repeat 2 times.
Sat: Rest.
Sun: 5k race!

The 5 weeks to 5k plan

	Mon	Tues	Weds	Thurs	Fri	Sat	Sun
Week 1	2-minute walk, 2-minute run. Repeat 5 times	Rest	2-minute walk, 2-minute run. Repeat 5 times	Rest	Rest	2-minute walk, 2-minute run. Repeat 5 times	Rest
Week 2	3-minute walk, 3-minute run. Repeat 4 times	Rest	3-minute walk, 3-minute run. Repeat 4 times	Rest	Rest	4-minute walk, 4-minute run. Repeat 4 times	Rest
Week 3	3-minute walk, 6-minute run. Repeat 3 times	Rest	3-minute walk, 6-minute run. Repeat 3 times	Rest	Rest	2-minute walk, 8-minute run. Repeat 3 times	Rest
Week 4	10-minute run, 1-minute walk. Repeat 3 times	Rest	10-minute run, 1-minute walk. Repeat 3 times	Rest	12-minute run, 3-minute walk. Repeat 2 times	Rest	15-minute run
Week 5	15-minute run, 1-minute walk. Repeat 2 times	Rest	10-minute run, 1-minute walk. Repeat 3 times	Rest	10-minute run, 1-minute walk. Repeat 2 times	Rest	5k Race!

Building Your Fitness – The 10 Weeks To 10K Plan

This next plan is for those that can comfortably run the 5k distance. If you've been following the 5k plan, then by now, your body should be getting used to running regularly, but the time it takes you to achieve this is going to be down to your individual fitness levels.

At this point, it's best to focus less on time and more on building your overall fitness. I'm a firm believer that if you put in the miles and keep running often, the times will improve by themselves. For some people, time is everything, and it can almost become an obsession to chisel off a few more seconds from your last run time. If this is what motivates you, then this is absolutely fine, just don't let it become something that starts to steal the enjoyment from what you're doing. If you're getting out there running, you're already winning, no matter what time you complete your run in.

The 10k distance (6.2 miles) is a really nice distance to run. It's probably why it's one of the most popular distances for amateur athletes. Globally, there are some huge races. The biggest currently is the Peachtree 10k Road Race in Atlanta, USA, which attracts over 55,000 runners[19]. Considered a long-distance race, it is long enough to test the body, but it isn't so far that you're going to be stressing your body in the same way that a half marathon does.

A 10k race was the first proper race that I entered after returning to running. This was about eight years ago now, and it was my first 10k in over five years. I was still building up my fitness levels, so I was certainly not in peak condition, and I can still remember the nerves on race-day morning. Lining up with all the other runners, lots of thoughts go through your head. "Am I too old to be doing this?", "Will I embarrass myself?", "Will I start too fast and then flake out?".

For the first-timers or the not-in-a-long-timers, it can be a daunting prospect.

When you have lots of longer runs under your belt, it's easy to underestimate how big a challenge the 10k distance is for those starting out. It's certainly a real benchmark achievement for many, but as with the 5k, it is very achievable.

In this section, we'll go through a 10-week plan to get you ready to run your first 10k. This plan is based on the assumption that you have already completed the 5k plan or can already comfortably run the 5k distance. This plan is designed for first-timers or those that haven't run a 10k in a long time. For those looking to get serious and start to run 10ks in under 40 minutes, I have included a separate section later on in this chapter.

The main difference with the 10k training is that we start to introduce different running speeds into the sessions. There are lots of baffling terms out there for different running speeds; fartlek, intervals, tempo and so on. Even a lot of dedicated runners get confused by these terms, and for now, it doesn't matter too much. The idea of these training plans is that they are simple to understand and easy to execute.

With that in mind, at this stage we'll introduce three different speeds; walking, easy runs, and steady runs.

Walking
The walking is to be used as a form of recovery between your running and will predominantly feature at the beginning of the plan while you build up your aerobic capacity.

Easy runs
Your easy runs should be jogging at a relaxed pace where you could comfortably have a conversation with someone running next to you without getting too out of breath.

<u>Steady runs</u>

For your steady runs, you should be running at a pace where conversation would be difficult. During steady runs, you'll notice your heart rate has increased and you'll be more focused on your exercise. To begin with, you may find it difficult to keep at your steady pace for long, but you'll soon build fitness and be able to maintain this pace for longer.

As before, we'll break each week down and look at what you need to do and why we are doing that. At the end of the section, you'll find a diagram that pulls the plan together in one place.

Week 1

For this first week, the focus is on easy running with recovery walks in 25-30-minute sessions. This will get your body used to running slightly longer distances with plenty of time to adjust.

Mon: 10-minute easy run, 5-minute walk, 5-minute easy run, 5-minute walk.
Tues: Rest.
Weds: 10-minute easy run, 5-minute walk, 10-minute easy run, 5-minute walk.
Thurs: Rest.
Fri: Rest.
Sat: 10-minute easy run, 5-minute walk, 10-minute easy run, 5-minute walk.
Sun: Rest.

Week 2

In your second week, you'll be steadily increasing your easy runs with lots of walking to help recovery. At the end of the week, you'll be aiming to complete a 20-minute easy run without stopping.

Mon: 12-minute easy run, 5-minute walk, 5-minute easy run, 5-minute walk.

Tues: Rest.
Weds: 12-minute easy run, 5-minute walk, 5-minute easy run, 5-minute walk.
Thurs: Rest.
Fri: Rest.
Sat: 5-minute walk, 20-minute easy run, 5-minute walk.
Sun: Rest.

Week 3

This week, you'll be doing your first steady running sessions. These may feel tough to start with but try and remember that each time you complete a steady run, you are extending your aerobic capacity and increasing your fitness.

Mon: 5-minute walk, 15-minute easy run, 5-minute walk.
Tues: Rest.
Weds: 5-minute easy run. 2-minute steady run, 1-minute walk repeated 5 times. 5-minute easy run.
Thurs: Rest.
Fri: Rest.
Sat: 5-minute walk, 20-minute easy run, 5-minute walk.
Sun: Rest.

Week 4

During week 4, you'll continue to build your stamina through your steady running sessions. You will also complete 40 minutes of easy running at the end of the week. Try and do this without stopping but feel free to walk if you need to.

Mon: 25-minute easy run.
Tues: Rest.
Weds: 5-minute easy run. 2-minute steady run, 1-minute walk repeated 5 times. 5-minute easy run.
Thurs: Rest.
Fri: Rest.
Sat: 40-minute easy run (walk if needed).

Sun: Rest.

Week 5
Now it's time to build up your overall weekly mileage. You'll do this by increasing your Monday run to 30 minutes and finishing the week by clocking up 60 minutes of combined running and walking.

Mon: 30-minute easy run.
Tues: Rest.
Weds: 5-minute easy run. 3-minute steady run, 1-minute walk repeated 5 times. 5-minute easy run.
Thurs: Rest.
Fri: Rest.
Sat: 20-minute easy run. 5-minute walk. 15-minute easy run. 5-minute walk. 15-minute easy run.
Sun: Rest.

Week 6
In week 6, you are going to be increasing your steady runs up to 5 minutes at a time. This may seem like a challenge at first, but as before, you'll have time to walk and recover between each steady run.

Mon: 35-minute easy run.
Tues: Rest.
Weds: 5-minute easy run. 5-minute steady run, 1-minute walk repeated 3 times. 5-minute easy run.
Thurs: Rest.
Fri: Rest.
Sat: 25-minute easy run. 5-minute walk. 15-minute easy run. 5-minute walk. 15-minute easy run.
Sun: Rest.

Week 7
This week you'll be building up the steady runs in the mid-week session to 4 repeats. At the end of the week, there is a 70-minute training session that mixes easy running and

walking to get your body used to exercising for longer.

Mon: 35-minute easy run.
Tues: Rest.
Weds: 5-minute easy run. 5-minute steady run, 1-minute walk repeated 4 times. 5-minute easy run.
Thurs: Rest.
Fri: Rest.
Sat: 25-minute easy run. 5-minute walk. 20-minute easy run. 5-minute walk. 15-minute easy run.
Sun: Rest.

Week 8

The jewel in the crown of this week's training is the 65-minute easy run at the end of the week. This is the first continuous run in the plan, but don't let it daunt you. You should attempt this at an easy pace, and you can always add a walking section if you need to.

Mon: 40-minute easy run.
Tues: Rest.
Weds: 10-minute easy run. 5-minute steady run, 30-second walk repeated 5 times. 5-minute easy run.
Thurs: Rest.
Fri: Rest.
Sat: 65-minute easy run (walk if needed).
Sun: Rest.

Week 9

This week you'll see that the distances start to decrease in preparation for the race. The mid-week run has a longer steady running session to try and build further on your maximum aerobic capacity.

Mon: 40-minute easy run.
Tues: Rest.
Weds: 15-minute easy run. 10-minute steady run, 1-minute walk repeated 2 times. 10-minute easy run.

Thurs: Rest.
Fri: Rest.
Sat: 55-minute easy run (walk if needed).
Sun: Rest.

Week 10

During this week, you'll start to taper off the training in preparation for race day. This is to ensure that you have plenty of energy reserves and so that your legs will be fresh and ready to run. Don't be tempted to do more miles than this; trust in the training you've put in.

Mon: 30-minute easy run.
Tues: Rest.
Weds: 20-minute easy run.
Thurs: Rest.
Fri: Rest.
Sat: 15-minute easy run.
Sun: 10k Race!

The 10 weeks to 10k Plan

	Mon	Tues	Weds	Thurs	Fri	Sat	Sun
Week 1	10-minute easy run, 5-minute walk, 5-minute easy run, 5-minute walk.	Rest	10-minute easy run, 5-minute walk, 10-minute easy run, 5-minute walk.	Rest	Rest	10-minute easy run, 5-minute walk, 10-minute easy run, 5-minute walk	Rest
Week 2	12-minute easy run, 5-minute walk, 5-minute easy run, 5-minute walk.	Rest	12-minute easy run, 5-minute walk, 5-minute easy run, 5-minute walk.	Rest	Rest	5-minute walk, 20-minute easy run, 5-minute walk.	Rest
Week 3	5-minute walk, 15-minute easy run, 5-minute walk.	Rest	5-minute easy run. 2-minute steady run, 1-minute walk repeated 5 times. 5-minute easy run.	Rest	Rest	5-minute walk, 20-minute easy run, 5-minute walk.	Rest
Week 4	25-minute easy run.	Rest	5-minute easy run. 2-minute steady run, 1-minute walk repeated 5 times. 5-minute easy run.	Rest	Rest	40-minute easy run (walk if needed).	Rest
Week 5	30-minute easy run.	Rest	5-minute easy run. 3-minute steady run, 1-minute walk repeated 5 times. 5-minute easy run.	Rest	Rest	20-minute easy run. 5-minute walk. 15-minute easy run. 5-minute walk. 15-minute easy run.	Rest
Week 6	35-minute easy run.	Rest	5-minute easy run. 5-minute steady run, 1-minute walk repeated 3 times. 5-minute easy run.	Rest	Rest	25-minute easy run. 5-minute walk. 15-minute easy run. 5-minute walk. 15-minute easy run.	Rest
Week 7	35-minute easy run.	Rest	5-minute easy run 5-minute steady run, 1-minute walk repeated 4 times. 5-minute easy run.	Rest	Rest	25-minute easy run. 5-minute walk. 20-minute easy run. 5-minute walk. 15-minute easy run.	Rest
Week 8	40-minute easy run.	Rest	10-minute easy run. 5-minute steady run, 30-second walk repeated 5 times. 5-minute easy run.	Rest	Rest	65-minute easy run (walk if needed).	Rest
Week 9	40-minute easy run.	Rest	15-minute easy run. 10-minute steady run, 1-minute walk repeated 2 times. 10-minute easy run.	Rest	Rest	55-minute easy run (walk if needed).	Rest
Week 10	30-minute easy run.	Rest	20-minute easy run.	Rest	Rest	15-minute easy run.	10k Race!

Pushing Your Limits – The 13 Weeks To 13 Miles Half Marathon Plan

Now things get a bit more serious. A half marathon distance (13.1 miles) is not to be sniffed at. This will be a considerable challenge for most people and will represent a real landmark achievement for many. Once you get to this sort of distance, you can no longer wing it or get away with missing sessions out of your training. It'll take dedication and commitment to be able to run this distance, but it is well worth the effort.

The half marathon distance will not only test your body more, but it will also test your mental strength. There is quite a psychological element to this distance, and that is because you are going to have to willingly put your body through discomfort to complete the course.

Everyone has their own experience when running a half marathon. For me, I always find the 8-mile and 10-mile points tough. The 8-mile point is probably due to the fact that you know you still have 5 miles to go, and the 10-mile point is down to having pushed my body to its limit for over an hour.

You may well have different points of the race where you'll have to overcome your own mental barriers. But, unless you're superhuman, you will have some tough moments. This is why the training is so important for this distance. We're not only training the body; we are also training the mind.

An interesting thing starts to happen as you begin to run longer and longer distances. Each time you run further, you expand your mental limits, as well as your physical limits. It's all about perspective. For example, the first time you run 1 mile, it seems a long way. But when you run 5 miles, 1 mile doesn't seem so far, and so it continues. Recently, when I've been training for a full marathon, I can be running anything up to 21 miles in training. Trust me, the first time you do this, it seems like a very, very long way, and it is. However, this has the effect of pushing your mental limits so that the next time you go for a 6-mile run, it literally feels like a walk in the park.

As we work through this half marathon plan, we'll be combining lots of different types of training, including hill workouts as well as cross-training. We'll also be building upon the different running speeds that we started to introduce in the 10k training plan. Following is a breakdown of each of these exercises and what they help accomplish.

Easy runs

These are runs that you can do at a relaxed pace. You should feel like you'd be able to hold a conversation with someone while running at this speed.

Steady runs

These runs are performed at a pace where conversation would be difficult. You should be pushing yourself but not going flat out.

Race pace runs

How quickly you'll want to run the race is going to be very personal to you. You can get a good idea of your ideal pace for the half marathon by using your 5k and 10k race times. As a general rule, you should add 30 seconds onto your 5k mile pace to get your 10k mile pace and then 30 seconds onto your 10k pace to get your half marathon pace. So, if you were running an 8-minute mile for the 5k, your half marathon pace would be a 9-minute mile.

Hill training

Hills are great for building up power in the legs and also rapidly increasing your aerobic capacity. You'll notice obvious gains from performing this exercise when you return to running on the flat. To begin with, find a hill with a gradual incline that will take you 45-60 seconds to climb. You can then ramp up the difficulty by finding steeper and longer hill sections to repeat.

Cross-training

What you do for your cross-training is going to be personal to you. Anything that builds your aerobic stamina is going to be beneficial. This can be cycling, swimming, walking or even circuit training in the gym. Personally, I like to mix up my running with cycling and a weekly circuit training session.

Week 1

The temptation when training for a longer race, such as the half marathon, can be to ramp up the miles too soon. But don't do it, or you could risk injury. Week 1 starts slowly so you can gradually build up your weekly miles. This week you'll be covering off 10 miles in 3 sessions.

Mon: 3-mile easy run.
Tues: Rest.
Weds: 3-mile easy run.
Thurs: Rest.
Fri: Rest.
Sat: 4-mile easy run.
Sun: Rest.
Total distance: 10 miles

Week 2

This week is similar in structure to Week 1 but ends with a slightly longer run on at the end of the week.

Mon: 3-mile easy run.
Tues: Rest.
Weds: 3-mile easy run.
Thurs: Rest.
Fri: Rest.
Sat: 6-mile easy run.
Sun: Rest.
Total distance: 12 miles

Week 3

This week the total mileage will remain the same, but there's an added cross-training session in the week to help build up overall fitness.

Mon: 3-mile easy run.
Tues: Rest.
Weds: 3-mile easy run.
Thurs: Cross-training.
Fri: Rest.
Sat: 6-mile easy run.
Sun: Rest.
Total distance: 12 miles

Week 4

During this week, there is a slight increase in weekly mileage to 15 miles with an introduction of a split easy and steady run mid-week. The cross-training session should now become a weekly feature of your training plan.

Mon: 3-mile easy run.
Tues: Rest.
Weds: 2-mile easy run. 2-mile steady run.
Thurs: Cross-training.
Fri: Rest.
Sat: 8-mile easy run
Sun: Rest.
Total distance: 15 miles

Week 5

This week has a slightly extended mid-week session with a slightly shorter end of week longer run. This is to give your body a little extra rest as it acclimatises to the previous week's long run.

Mon: 4-mile easy run.
Tues: Rest.
Weds: 2-mile easy run. 2-mile steady run. 2-mile easy run.
Thurs: Cross-training.

Fri: Rest.
Sat: 6-mile easy run.
Sun: Rest.
Total distance: 16 miles

Week 6

Now you are going to introduce some hill runs into your schedule. These will help you build up your endurance. The end of the week will see your longest run yet at 9 miles.

Mon: 4-mile easy run.
Tues: Rest.
Weds: Hill runs. Find a gradual incline with a 45-60-second climb and repeat ascending and descending for 5 miles.
Thurs: Cross-training.
Fri: Rest.
Sat: 9-mile easy run.
Sun: Rest.
Total distance: 18 miles

Week 7

This week you'll complete a 6-mile run at your race pace. This is great for getting your mind, as well as your body, ready to run for longer at this speed. Your long run at the end of the week will consist of a mixture of easy and steady running.

Mon: 4-mile easy run.
Tues: Rest.
Weds: 1-mile easy run. 6 miles at race pace.
Thurs: Cross-training.
Fri: Rest.
Sat: 2-mile easy run. 3-mile steady run. 2-mile easy run.
Sun: Rest.
Total distance: 18 miles

Week 8

For this week, try and find a slightly steeper and more challenging hill climb that you can repeat over 6 miles. To end the week, there's a 9-mile easy long run. This will be a significant challenge, so make sure you go at a pace that you feel comfortable with.

Mon: 4-mile easy run.
Tues: Rest.
Weds: Hill runs. Find a steeper incline with a 60-second climb and repeat ascending and descending for 6 miles.
Thurs: Cross-training.
Fri: Rest.
Sat: 9-mile easy run.
Sun: Rest.
Total distance: 19 miles

Week 9

With a weekly mileage increase to 22 miles, you're now starting to hit the peak of your training plan. The mid-week session has extended intervals at race pace with a mix of easy and steady running to finish the week.

Mon: 3-mile easy run.
Tues: Rest.
Weds: 2-mile easy run. 3 miles at race pace. 2-mile easy run. 3 miles at race pace.
Thurs: Cross-training.
Fri: Rest.
Sat: 2-mile easy run. 5-mile steady run. 2-mile easy run.
Sun: Rest.
Total distance: 22 miles

Week 10

The main focus points for Week 10 are another hill training session followed by a 10-mile long run at an easy pace. This is the furthest that you will run in training and should give you confidence that you're then just 5k short of the full race distance.

Mon: 4-mile easy run.

Tues: Rest.

Weds: Hill runs. Find a steep incline with a 60-second climb and repeat ascending and descending for 6 miles.

Thurs: Cross-training.

Fri: Rest.

Sat: 10-mile easy run

Sun: Rest.

Total distance: 20 miles

Week 11

In week 11, the sessions are designed to keep your fitness at its peak before we start to taper off the miles ahead of the race.

Mon: 4-mile easy run.

Tues: Rest.

Weds: 2-mile easy run. 5 miles at race pace. 1-mile easy run.

Thurs: Cross-training.

Fri: Rest.

Sat: 2-mile easy run. 6-mile steady run. 2-mile easy run.

Sun: Rest.

Total distance: 22 miles

Week 12

In week 12, there's a gradual taper ready for the race. You'll still be covering off 20 miles over the week with a 7-miler at race pace mid-week.

Mon: 3-mile easy run.

Tues: Rest.

Weds: 7 miles at race pace.

Thurs: Cross-training.

Fri: Rest.

Sat: 9-mile easy run.

Sun: Rest.

Total distance: 20 miles

Week 13

Well done on completing your half marathon training plan. Now, it's race week, so it's time to get those last few runs in. You'll start the week with a steady run and then rapidly taper off to some easy runs ahead of race day. There's a short 30-minute shake-out run the day before the race that's good for keeping the muscles tuned ready. On race day, try and wake up early to have your breakfast in good time before you start. Aim to eat 2.5 hours before and hydrate modestly. Over-hydration can be a bigger problem than dehydration, so don't go downing pint after pint of water. They'll always be plenty of water stations on the route.

Mon: 3-mile steady run.
Tues: Rest.
Weds: 2-mile easy run. 2 miles at race pace.
Thurs: Rest.
Fri: Rest.
Sat: 30-minute easy run.
Sun: Half Marathon Race!
Total distance: Approximately 24 miles

The 13 weeks to 13 miles Half Marathon Plan	Mon	Tues	Weds	Thurs	Fri	Sat	Sun
Week 1 Total distance: 10 miles	3-mile easy run	Rest	3-mile easy run	Rest	Rest	4-mile easy run	Rest
Week 2 Total distance: 12 miles	3-mile easy run	Rest	3-mile easy run	Rest	Rest	6-mile easy run	Rest
Week 3 Total distance: 12 miles	3-mile easy run	Rest	3-mile easy run	Cross-training	Rest	6-mile easy run	Rest
Week 4 Total distance: 15 miles	3-mile easy run	Rest	2-mile easy run. 2-mile steady run.	Cross-training	Rest	8-mile easy run	Rest
Week 5 Total distance: 16 miles	4-mile easy run	Rest	2-mile easy run. 2-mile steady run. 2-mile easy run.	Cross-training	Rest	6-mile easy run	Rest
Week 6 Total distance: 18 miles	4-mile easy run	Rest	Hill runs. Find a gradual incline with a 45-60-second climb and repeat ascending and descending for 5 miles.	Cross-training	Rest	9-mile easy run	Rest
Week 7 Total distance: 18 miles	4-mile easy run	Rest	1-mile easy run. 6 miles at race pace.	Cross-training	Rest	2-mile easy run. 3-mile steady run. 2-mile easy run.	Rest
Week 8 Total distance: 19 miles	9-mile easy run	Rest	Hill runs. Find a steeper incline with a 60-second climb and repeat ascending and descending for 6 miles.	Cross-training	Rest	9-mile easy run	Rest
Week 9 Total distance: 22 miles	3-mile easy run	Rest	2-mile easy run. 3 miles at race pace. 2-mile easy run. 3 miles at race pace.	Cross-training	Rest	2-mile easy run. 5-mile steady run. 2-mile easy run.	Rest
Week 10 Total distance: 20 miles	4-mile easy run	Rest	Hill runs. Find a steep incline with a 60-second climb and repeat ascending and descending for 6 miles.	Cross-training	Rest	10-mile easy run	Rest
Week 11 Total distance: 22 miles	4-mile easy run	Rest	2-mile easy run. 5 miles at race pace. 1-mile easy run.	Cross-training	Rest	2-mile easy run. 6-mile steady run. 2-mile easy run.	Rest
Week 12 Total distance: 20 miles	3-mile easy run	Rest	7 miles at race pace.	Cross-training	Rest	9-mile easy run.	Rest
Week 13 Total distance: 24 miles	3-mile steady run	Rest	2-mile easy run. 2 miles at race pace.	Rest	Rest	30-minute easy run.	Half Marathon Race!

Realising Your Targets – Advanced Plans

This part of the book isn't for everyone. For many, it is enough of an achievement to get yourself around a 10k or a half marathon. But for some, and I include myself in this, there is a certain thrill in pushing your body past its comfort zone. I enjoy the competition with myself and others, and I find that aiming for specific targets in races helps to add that edge of motivation to my training.

I also want to make it clear here, as I did at the beginning of the chapter, that I don't claim to be the world's leading authority on reaching these times. This is written from the perspective of a very normal amateur athlete who has reached targets that he once felt were completely impossible. I'm including this section as I want to share my experience and methods for having hit these targets, as I think this will be interesting to other amateurs in a similar position.

My journey to a sub-40-minute 10k

When I did my 10k after many years of not running, I managed to clock in a 45 minute 42 seconds. It's an okay-ish time, but I remember that I felt like this was at my physical limit. What really piqued my interest was how many older runners were blazing past me during the last 3k. Afterwards, when the results came in, I had a good look through the top 50 runners, and I was amazed to see that there were lots of people in their 40s, 50s, and 60s clocking in times close to, or below, the 40-minute mark.

This really fired up my motivation to try and get faster. My thinking was that if these older ladies and gents could do it, then so could I.

Then, as I suspect many others do, I went completely the wrong way about it. In my naivety, I thought I would get faster by training at race pace for as long as I could keep it up. And no surprises, it didn't work. After months of trying, I was only fractionally faster than before. I felt like I was missing some big secret here, after all, how could all those other older runners be so fast?

It was then that I started doing my research online and really getting geeky with reading training plans and blogs by those amateurs that had snuck under the 40-minute mark.

By using and adapting these plans, I started introducing speed workouts into my training as well as increasing the distance of my long runs. Suddenly, things started to drop into place, and I was chiselling chunks off my training times.

Feeling pretty confident, I entered my next 10k race. I went out fast for the first 3k, definitely too quick, and then clung on for dear life for the next 7k of the race. This time I finished in 41 minutes 37 seconds. Much better than my first attempt but still a way off the sub-40-minute time. And again, I felt like I was running at my absolute peak.

It was time for a re-think, so I decided to increase the frequency of my runs hoping that this would help. This seemed to be working, and yet more seconds were coming off my mile times with the fastest in the region of 6m 20s per mile. Hoping that the excitement of race day would inspire me below the 40-minute milestone, I entered my next 10k. This time I came in at 41 minutes 5 seconds. Fractionally better than the last race.

It was at this stage that my mind started telling me, "You're just too old to do this." and "Maybe if you were 25, you could stand a chance.". But being determined to do this, I re-evaluated my approach, and it was then that I read about the benefits of increasing core strength and adding circuit training to the mix.

Having been solely focused on running, this initially seemed at odds. Could I really get better at running by doing non-running exercise? I decided to give it a go.

I added a self-composed circuit training workout to my overall weekly plan and also core strength-building exercises (you can see the full breakdown of my regime at the end of this section). Almost straight away, I felt the benefits. Suddenly I could clock up 6m 15s miles in my training, and I felt much stronger overall.

I decided to sign up for the Brighton Winter 10k, a very refreshing and fast course right on the seafront. This time, right from the start it felt good. I was running at my peak but felt I could keep going. I was comfortable in my uncomfortableness. Checking the watch, I could see that I was hitting each kilometre on or below the 4-minute mark – things were looking good. By 8k, it was starting to hurt but I could draw enough incentive to keep up the pace from the knowledge that I was still on target.

The satisfaction and thrill of seeing the timer still in the 30s as I approached the finish were immense, and I crossed the line in 39 minutes 49 seconds. At last, I'd done it. I was shattered but very proud of myself. This marked a real high point in my six years back to fitness. It also proved to me that, whatever my mind was telling me before, it simply wasn't true. I was capable of hitting a time that was unimaginable to me just three years before when I clocked up my 45-minuter. This new time put me in the top 4.5% fastest runners in the UK. Not bad for a 39-year-old.

This was a real turning point for me. I was now full of confidence and ready for even bigger goals. The interesting thing is that when you've gone sub-40-minutes once, it seems to remove a barrier in your mind. So the next time I did a 10k, I managed to hit 39 minutes and 30 seconds – and it felt pretty good. I was getting older and faster.

Advanced Plans – The Sub-40-Minute 10K Plan

There is no such thing as one plan fits all. I certainly found this to be the case when I was religiously following plans and then still not hitting the sub-40 goal. Everyone is different and our bodies respond to different things. I have developed the plan that follows based on what has worked for me, but I've also tried to make it broad enough that it's likely to work for you too. As with anything, if you're following it and you're still not hitting your target, give it a nudge and an adjustment to your needs. I'm a believer in intuition. My intuition told me I needed to improve my overall body strength, and that worked for me. Maybe for you, your body's core strength is good, but you need to increase your speed workouts. The key piece of advice here is, don't be afraid to experiment.

With this in mind, I'd advise using the plan below as your base plan to build on and adjust to your needs. Your body will tell you what is working for you, all you need to do is listen. This plan is only six weeks long. This is because it assumes you already have a good base level of running fitness before you attempt it. You should be able to comfortably run a sub-7-minute mile. If not, keep up your general training until you can do this.

This plan includes the following types of training:

Easy runs
These are runs that you can do at a relaxed pace. You should feel like you'd be able to hold a conversation with someone while running at this speed.

Steady runs
These runs are performed at a pace where conversation would be difficult. You should be pushing yourself but not going flat out.

Race pace runs
For a sub-40-minute 10k, you'll need to be averaging a pace just below 6 minutes and 26 seconds a mile, so this will need to be your goal race pace.

Fast runs
Your fast runs should be at a pace that's faster than your race pace. In the shorter fast runs of 2 minutes and under, this will mean going flat out. For longer fast runs of 10 minutes or more, it may be a touch slower, but you should still be running at your maximum with your heart rate near the maximum for your age range. As an example, my maximum heart rate is 180 bpm for my

age range, and during my fast runs, my heart rate averages 172 bpm.

Maximum heart rate by age:

20 years	200 bpm
30 years	190 bpm
35 years	185 bpm
40 years	180 bpm
45 years	175 bpm
50 years	170 bpm
55 years	165 bpm
60 years	160 bpm
65 years	155 bpm
70 years	150 bpm

Hill training

Hills are great for building up power in the legs and also rapidly increasing your aerobic capacity. You'll notice obvious gains from performing this exercise when you return to running on the flat. To begin with, find a hill with a gradual incline that will take you 45-60 seconds to climb. You can then ramp up the difficulty by finding steeper and longer hill sections to repeat.

Circuit training

I'd advise a 45-minute circuit training session in the gym to build your core strength and overall fitness. This can be adapted based on your needs. I'd recommend the following as a starting point:

- 7 minutes on the rowing machine
- 8 minutes of core exercises with intervals of planks, press-ups, sit-ups, abdominal curls
- 5 minutes of weight training with dumbbell repetitions
- 15 minutes on the elliptical machine set to medium difficulty; 1 minute at 55rpm, 1 minute at 65rpm, 1 minute at 75rpm, 1 minute at 85rpm, 1 minute at

100rpm+. Repeat 3 times.

- 10 minutes on the treadmill; 2 minutes at 8-minute miles, 2 minutes at 7-minute miles, 2 minutes at 6:30-minute miles, 2 minutes at 6-minute miles, 2 minutes at 8-minute miles

As before, we'll start with the weekly breakdown of the plan, and then this will be followed by the diagram of the complete plan.

Week 1
Mon: 2-minute fast run, 4-minute steady run. Repeat 3 times.
Tues: 15-minute easy run. 15-minute steady run. 15-minute easy run.
Weds: 60-minute easy run.
Thurs: Circuit training session.
Fri: Rest.
Sat: 10-minute easy run. 10-minute steady run. 10-minute fast run. 10-minute steady run. 10-minute easy run.
Sun: 70-minute easy run.

Week 2
Mon: 2-minute fast run, 4-minute steady run. Repeat 3 times.
Tues: 5-minute easy run, 5-minute fast run. Repeat 4 times.
Weds: 45-minute easy run.
Thurs: Circuit training session.
Fri: Rest.
Sat: 10-minute easy run. 10-minute steady run. 10-minute fast run. 10-minute steady run. 10-minute easy run.
Sun: 80-minute easy run.

Week 3
Mon: 2-minute fast run, 4-minute steady run. Repeat 3 times.
Tues: 15-minute easy run. 15-minute steady run. 15-minute

easy run.

Weds: 30-minute easy run.

Thurs: Hill run. Find a hill will a 60-second climb and ascend and descend for 4 miles.

Fri: Rest.

Sat: 5k park run at race pace.

Sun: 90-minute easy run.

Week 4

Mon: 2-minute fast run, 4-minute steady run. Repeat 3 times.

Tues: 5-minute easy run, 5-minute fast run. Repeat 4 times.

Weds: 45-minute easy run.

Thurs: Circuit training session.

Fri: Rest.

Sat: 10-minute easy run. 10-minute steady run. 10-minute fast run. 10-minute steady run. 10-minute easy run.

Sun: 70-minute easy run.

Week 5

Mon: 2-minute fast run, 4-minute steady run. Repeat 3 times.

Tues: 15-minute easy run. 15-minute steady run. 15-minute easy run.

Weds: 30-minute easy run.

Thurs: Hill run. Find a hill will a 60-second climb and ascend and descend for 4 miles.

Fri: Rest.

Sat: 5k park run at race pace.

Sun: 90-minute easy run.

Week 6

Mon: 2-minute fast run, 4-minute steady run. Repeat 3 times.

Tues: 5-minute easy run, 5-minute fast run. Repeat 4 times.

Weds: 40-minute easy run.

Thurs: 2-minute fast run, 4-minute steady run. Repeat 3

times.
Fri: 30-minute easy run.
Sat: 20-minute easy run.
Sun: 10k Race!

	Mon	Tues	Weds	Thurs	Fri	Sat	Sun
The sub-40-minute 10k plan							
Week 1	2-minute fast run, 4-minute steady run. Repeat 3 times.	15-minute easy run. 15-minute steady run. 15-minute easy run.	60-minute easy run.	Circuit training session.	Rest	10-minute easy run. 10-minute steady run. 10-minute fast run. 10-minute steady run. 10-minute easy run.	70-minute easy run.
Week 2	2-minute fast run, 4-minute steady run. Repeat 3 times.	5-minute easy run, 5-minute fast run. Repeat 4 times.	45-minute easy run.	Circuit training session.	Rest	10-minute easy run. 10-minute steady run. 10-minute fast run. 10-minute steady run. 10-minute easy run.	80-minute easy run.
Week 3	2-minute fast run, 4-minute steady run. Repeat 3 times.	15-minute easy run. 15-minute steady run. 15-minute easy run.	30-minute easy run.	Hill run. Find a hill will a 60-second climb and ascend and descend for 4 miles.	Rest	5k park run at race pace.	90-minute easy run.
Week 4	2-minute fast run, 4-minute steady run. Repeat 3 times.	5-minute easy run, 5-minute fast run. Repeat 4 times.	45-minute easy run.	Circuit training session.	Rest	10-minute easy run. 10-minute steady run. 10-minute fast run. 10-minute steady run. 10-minute easy run.	70-minute easy run.
Week 5	2-minute fast run, 4-minute steady run. Repeat 3 times.	15-minute easy run. 15-minute steady run. 15-minute easy run.	30-minute easy run.	Hill run. Find a hill will a 60-second climb and ascend and descend for 4 miles.	Rest	5k park run at race pace.	90-minute easy run.
Week 6	2-minute fast run, 4-minute steady run. Repeat 3 times.	5-minute easy run, 5-minute fast run. Repeat 4 times.	40-minute easy run.	2-minute fast run, 4-minute steady run. Repeat 3 times.	30-minute easy run.	20-minute easy run.	10k Race!

Advanced Plans – The Sub-90-Minute Half Marathon Plan

If you can run a sub-40-minute 10k, you may also think it's then easy to hit a sub-90-minute half marathon, but it's not quite that simple. The techniques that you've learnt doing your 10k training will certainly help, however, these are two quite different disciplines at this pace range.

Whereas the 10k distance is all about speed, the half marathon is a combination of speed and endurance. In a 10k, I feel like I'm going as fast as I can for as long as I can – with a feeling of hanging on for dear life for the last 2 km. In contrast, the half marathon requires a lot of strategy and discipline to make sure you don't start too fast and that you don't drift off mentally and lose pace through the race.

This element of strategy makes the half marathon my favourite race distance. Physically, it's also the distance I'm most suited to. Thanks to a DNA test, I know I have predominantly fast-twitch muscle fibres. This muscle make-up is great for sprinting and mid-distance races but is not as suited to marathons and above. This would explain why my current personal best marathon time is 3 hours 40 mins (although it was very hilly!), whereas my half marathon best is 1 hour 29 mins.

Half marathon training for this time target is going to include a mix of longer, slower runs, as well as short, fast interval training. As with the sub 40-minute 10k plan, it also requires some time in the gym to train your core and strengthen the body through circuit training.

This plan includes the following types of training:

Easy runs
These are runs that you can do at a relaxed pace. You should

feel like you'd be able to hold a conversation with someone while running at this speed.

Steady runs
These runs are performed at a pace where conversation would be difficult. You should be pushing yourself but not going flat out.

Race pace runs
For a sub-90-minute half marathon, you'll need to be averaging a pace just below 6 minutes and 52 seconds a mile, so this will need to be your goal race pace.

Fast runs
Your fast runs should be at a pace that's faster than your race pace. In the shorter fast runs of 2 minutes and under, this will mean going flat out. For longer fast runs of 10 minutes or more, it may be a touch slower, but you should still be running at your maximum with your heart rate near the maximum for your age range (see the sub-40-minute 10k plan for further details).

Hill training
Hills are great for building up power in the legs and also rapidly increasing your aerobic capacity. You'll notice obvious gains from performing this exercise when you return to running on the flat. To begin with, find a hill with a gradual incline that will take you 60 seconds to climb. You can then ramp up the difficulty by finding steeper and longer hill sections to repeat.

Circuit training
I'd advise a 45-minute circuit training session in the gym to build your core strength and overall fitness. This can be adapted based on your needs. I'd recommend the following as a starting point.

- 7 minutes on the rowing machine
- 8 minutes of core exercises with intervals of planks, press-ups, sit-ups, stomach crunches
- 5 minutes of weight training with dumbbell repeti-

tions

- 15 minutes on the elliptical machine set to medium difficulty; 1 minute at 55rpm, 1 minute at 65rpm, 1 minute at 75rpm, 1 minute at 85rpm, 1 minute at 100rpm+. Repeat 3 times.
- 10 minutes on the treadmill; 2 minutes at 8-minute miles, 2 minutes at 7-minute miles, 2 minutes at 6:30-minute miles, 2 minutes at 6-minute miles, 2 minutes at 8-minute miles.

As before, we'll start with the weekly breakdown of the plan, and then this will be followed by the diagram of the complete plan.

Week 1
Mon: 40-minute easy run
Tues: 2-minute easy run, 2-minute fast run. Repeat 5 times.
Weds: 30-minute easy run.
Thurs: Circuit training session.
Fri: Rest.
Sat: 10-minute easy run. 10-minute steady run. 10-minute fast run. Repeat 2 times.
Sun: 65-minute easy run.

Week 2
Mon: 20-minute easy run. 20-minute steady run.
Tues: 2-minute easy run, 2-minute fast run. Repeat 5 times.
Weds: 40-minute easy run. 5-minute fast run.
Thurs: Circuit training session.
Fri: Rest.
Sat: 10-minute easy run. 40-minute steady run. 10-minute easy run.
Sun: 65-minute easy run.

Week 3
Mon: 20-minute easy run. 20-minute steady run. 5-minute fast.

Tues: 2-minute easy run, 3-minute fast run. Repeat 5 times.
Weds: Hill run. Find a hill will a 60-second climb and ascend and descend for 4 miles.
Thurs: Circuit training session.
Fri: Rest.
Sat: 10-minute easy run. 10-minute steady run. 10-minute fast run. Repeat 2 times.
Sun: 75-minute easy run.

Week 4
Mon: 45-minute easy run.
Tues: 2-minute easy run, 3-minute fast run. Repeat 5 times.
Weds: 10-minute easy run. 10-minute steady run. 10-minute fast run. 10-minute easy run.
Thurs: Circuit training session.
Fri: Rest.
Sat: 10-minute easy run. 40-minute steady run. 10-minute easy run.
Sun: 95-minute easy run.

Week 5
Mon: 20-minute easy run. 20-minute steady run. 5-minute fast.
Tues: 2-minute easy run, 3-minute fast run. Repeat 5 times.
Weds: Hill run. Find a hill will a 60-second climb and ascend and descend for 4 miles.
Thurs: Circuit training session.
Fri: Rest.
Sat: 10-minute easy run. 10-minute steady run. 10-minute fast run. Repeat 2 times.
Sun: 75-minute easy run.

Week 6
Mon: 45-minute easy run.
Tues: 2-minute easy run, 5-minute fast run. Repeat 3 times.
Weds: 10-minute easy run. 10-minute steady run. 10-minute fast run. 10-minute easy run.

Thurs: Circuit training session.
Fri: Rest.
Sat: 10-minute easy run. 40-minute steady run. 10-minute easy run.
Sun: 95-minute easy run.

Week 7
Mon: 40-minute easy run. 5-minute fast run.
Tues: 2-minute easy run, 5-minute fast run. Repeat 4 times.
Weds: 10-minute steady run. 10-minute fast run. 10-minute easy run.
Thurs: Circuit training session.
Fri: Rest.
Sat: 30-minute easy run.
Sun: 10km race (aim for sub 40-minutes).

Week 8
Mon: 40-minute steady run. 5-minute fast run.
Tues: 2-minute easy run, 5-minute fast run. Repeat 4 times.
Weds: Hill run. Find a hill will a 60-second climb and ascend and descend for 4 miles.
Thurs: Circuit training session.
Fri: Rest.
Sat: 10-minute easy run. 10-minute steady run. 10-minute fast run. Repeat 2 times.
Sun: 95-minute easy run.

Week 9
Mon: 45-minute easy run.
Tues: 2-minute easy run, 5-minute fast run. Repeat 4 times.
Weds: 10-minute steady run. 10-minute fast run. 10-minute easy run.
Thurs: Circuit training session.
Fri: Rest.
Sat: 30-minute easy run.
Sun: 15-minute easy run. 10-minute steady run. 10-minute fast run. Repeat 2 times.

Week 10

Mon: Circuit training session.

Tues: 2-minute easy run, 5-minute fast run. Repeat 4 times.

Weds: 45-minute easy run.

Thurs: 10-minute steady run. 10-minute fast run. 10-minute easy run.

Fri: Rest.

Sat: 30-minute easy run.

Sun: Half Marathon Race!

The sub-90-minute half marathon plan

	Mon	Tues	Weds	Thurs	Fri	Sat	Sun
Week 1	40-minute easy run	2-minute easy run, 2-minute fast run. Repeat 5 times.	30-minute easy run.	Circuit training session.	Rest	10-minute easy run. 10-minute steady run. 10-minute fast run. Repeat 2 times.	65-minute easy run.
Week 2	20-minute easy run. 20-minute steady run.	2-minute easy run, 2-minute fast run. Repeat 5 times.	40-minute easy run. 5-minute fast run.	Circuit training session.	Rest	10-minute easy run. 40-minute steady run. 10-minute easy run.	65-minute easy run.
Week 3	20-minute easy run. 20-minute steady run. 5-minute fast.	2-minute easy run, 3-minute fast run. Repeat 5 times.	Hill run. Find a hill will a 60-second climb and ascend and descend for 4 miles.	Circuit training session.	Rest	10-minute easy run. 10-minute steady run. 10-minute fast run. Repeat 2 times.	75-minute easy run.
Week 4	45-minute easy run.	2-minute easy run, 3-minute fast run. Repeat 5 times.	10-minute easy run. 10-minute steady run. 10-minute fast run. 10-minute easy run.	Circuit training session.	Rest	10-minute easy run. 40-minute steady run. 10-minute easy run.	95-minute easy run.
Week 5	20-minute easy run. 20-minute steady run. 5-minute fast.	2-minute easy run, 3-minute fast run. Repeat 5 times.	Hill run. Find a hill will a 60-second climb and ascend and descend for 4 miles.	Circuit training session.	Rest	10-minute easy run. 10-minute steady run. 10-minute fast run. Repeat 2 times.	75-minute easy run.
Week 6	45-minute easy run.	2-minute easy run, 5-minute fast run. Repeat 3 times.	10-minute easy run. 10-minute steady run. 10-minute fast run. 10-minute easy run.	Circuit training session.	Rest	10-minute easy run. 40-minute steady run. 10-minute easy run.	95-minute easy run.
Week 7	40-minute easy run. 5-minute fast run.	2-minute easy run, 5-minute fast run. Repeat 4 times.	10-minute steady run. 10-minute fast run. 10-minute easy run.	Circuit training session.	Rest	30-minute easy run.	10km race (aim for sub 40-minutes)
Week 8	40-minute steady run. 5-minute fast.	2-minute easy run, 5-minute fast run. Repeat 4 times.	Hill run. Find a hill will a 60-second climb and ascend and descend for 4 miles.	Circuit training session.	Rest	10-minute easy run. 10-minute steady run. 10-minute fast run. Repeat 2 times.	95-minute easy run.
Week 9	45-minute easy run.	2-minute easy run, 5-minute fast run. Repeat 4 times.	10-minute steady run. 10-minute fast run. 10-minute easy run.	Circuit training session.	Rest	30-minute easy run.	15-minute easy run. 10-minute steady run. 10-minute fast run. Repeat 2 times.
Week 10	Circuit training session.	2-minute easy run, 5-minute fast run. Repeat 4 times.	45-minute easy run.	10-minute steady run. 10-minute fast run. 10-minute easy run.	Rest	30-minute easy run.	Half Marathon Race!

CHAPTER 9

Run to overcome

Overcoming Injury

We all have to accept that at some point, we'll get injured. Whether it's an injury that you get from running or from some other unfortunate accident, it can have the same effect – no running.

This can be extremely frustrating, especially when you have established a regular running routine or constructed a carefully designed training plan.

The most important thing to remember is not to try and train or run through the injury. Your first port of call should be to visit your doctor. They will usually be able to refer you to a good physio. If not, or you're in a hurry, book yourself to see a physio specialising in running injuries. You'll be surprised how many there are out there, and they are probably not as expensive as you might assume.

I had my own experience of injury while training for the 2019 Bournemouth Marathon. I was still five months out from race day, and my training was going well. While mid-way through a Sunday 12-mile run, I had a dull ache down the inside of my right calf that travelled down to my foot. Because it wasn't a sharp pain, I tried to stretch it out and carried on running. This was a big mistake.

I got home, not thinking much of it, had a stretch out and went for a shower. Afterwards, I had a closer look at my lower leg and noticed it was starting to swell up. By evening it had lost all definition around the ankle and looked like an elephant's foot. This was not good.

I booked in to see a physio and found out I had torn my plantar facia and had what's known as plantar fasciitis. For a runner, this is very bad news. The usual recovery is at least four weeks and can be up to twelve weeks for more serious cases.

Luckily, I was more at the four-week end of the scale. Probably also thanks to a great physio and intensive recovery exercises. A month later I was back to slow jogging and eight weeks after injury, I was back to my normal training intensity. It did blow a massive hole in my plans, but I still managed to complete the Bournemouth Marathon in 3 hours 41 minutes. Not too bad considering the training gap.

When injury strikes like this, it can be tempting to sit on the sofa and sulk. Needless to say, this won't help. Not only will your fitness slide, but you'll also be missing your regular endorphin hit and start to feel more down than usual. Instead, I'd recommend positive action. Ask your physio what exercises you may be able to do. Preferably find an activity that will keep your cardiovascular fitness levels up. If it's an injury to the legs, then non-load-bearing exercises such as swimming or even cycling could work.

I found that I was still able to use the cross-trainer machine at the gym while I was injured, so I replaced the miles with more minutes at the gym. It wasn't quite the same, but it meant that when I returned to running, my cardiovascular fitness was still relatively good, and it was much easier to step things back up.

If you have a really major injury and it requires complete rest, I'd recommend reading some inspirational running books or watching some films about endurance athletes. This will help keep you motivated for your return, and you'll also advance your knowledge as a runner and be able to put some of that into practice on your return.

Scientific research has actually found that thanks to what's called 'mirror neurons' that allow us to empathise with others, simply watching sport can activate the same areas of the brain as it does for those taking part. So, even though we aren't physically participating, we are experiencing the same feelings at a neurological level. We have all experienced this to some degree when, for example, wincing while watching two players clash heads in a football game. The good news is that it means even when we can't train the body, we can still train the brain by watching someone else play sport. Sometimes, this can be enough to keep us in the right mindset and ready to start running again[20].

Above all, when you have an injury, try and stay positive. Even if you had your sights set on a big race, remember there will be plenty of others. The important thing is not to do any long-term damage to your body.

Overcoming Slumps

So, you've created your sustainable plan, you've been diligently racking up the miles and going through all your usual training, and then, all of a sudden, you hit a motivational slump.

These slumps will happen at some point. Even top athletes experience these. Having watched the Usain Bolt documentary, I am Bolt, I was struck by how hard he found it to keep up his training. At points, it seemed that this was actually the biggest hurdle he had to overcome as he strived to stay at the top.

I wonder if this had a psychological element. After all, he had achieved everything in his chosen running disciplines. He was undisputedly the best. What else did he really have to prove by doing it again and again?

Although few of us are ever going to have the problem of remaining the fastest person on the planet, I think that sometimes similar psychology may be at play when it comes to our own slumps. I know that some of my own motivation issues came after I had hit my own time goals in 10ks and half marathons. Where do you go from these personal successes?

It's important at these moments to reset your goals and look for fresh challenges. For me, this has led me to explore different types of running, such as trail running.

Sometimes, slumps in motivation can just happen out of the blue with no relation to anything you've done. I've also experienced a good few of these and they really do become a battle between the mind and the body. In the summer of 2018, I hit one of these speedbumps. It was strange as I'd had a productive start to the year and completed some great races but come the middle of the year, I was struggling to get out and train. I wasn't ill, and I wasn't overly tired or stressed, but it felt like someone had strapped lead boots to my feet. My inner voice was also starting to chip in unhelpful advice such as "Come on, you've achieved the times you wanted, maybe it's time to take it easy." and the old chestnut of "You're getting too old to be doing this.".

Everyone has their own methods of dealing with times like these. Mine was to keep going. I ran through the slump. It's not easy, but after about eight weeks of this I came out the other side, importantly, without a huge hole blown in my training calendar. I have now developed a good method for dealing with unhelpful thoughts. I do the opposite of what my negative thoughts tell me. If it tells me to slow down, I speed up. If it says 8 miles is too far today, I try and do 10 miles. This may sound silly, but it actually works to quieten the negativity. The mind soon learns that complaining equals more training.

If you are hit by your own slump, as well as sticking to your training, I'd encourage you to evaluate what you've enjoyed from your running experience. Maybe it's the camaraderie of running with others, or maybe it's that alone time to do your own thing?

If challenges are your thing, set some new ones. There are lots of companies offering running holidays now so that you can experience new places and find new friends. Globally, there is also a growing trend for running festivals which can also help you to meet with the wider running community.

The old adage that a change is as good as a rest is true here as well. In fact, when it comes to running, a change of scenery is much better than a rest.

CHAPTER 10

Measuring your progress

I really hope the stories in this book, along with the training plans, have helped you to begin your own running adventure and establish a sustainable routine. So, what's next? Well, the more you run, the more you begin to realise that running doesn't have a destination. Of course, there are milestones and achievements along the way, but really, it's a journey of exploration and an on-going work in progress for your fitness.

However, what is important every now and then, is to stop and reflect on what you've achieved so far. This is a great thing to do every few months because it is often easy to overlook how far you have come when the changes happen so incrementally over days and weeks. Just as we can be surprised by how unfit we have become in a matter of months, the same is true of positive changes to our health.

Having now been running very regularly for nearly a decade, the changes in my fitness from today to when I first started are huge. I never imagined I would be capable of running a marathon or any of the other things I have achieved. But I also remember how slow the progress was in those early months and how I was frustrated that my fitness seemed slow to improve. With the benefit of hindsight, I can now clearly see that progress was being made but that it takes time – many months in reality. But once you do the right training, and stick with it, the positive changes will always follow.

Following are some things that you can do right away to help you see how far you have come already. I would only recommend doing these if you have been sticking to your training for 3-6 months, if not, then revisit these once you have your routine more established. And remember, there are no set goals that you must achieve by certain points. Everybody is different, and we all respond to running differently. So, be patient with yourself, and if you haven't seen the results you expected, keep at it. You will reach them.

Evaluate your state of mind

It's very easy to focus too much on the physical goals we want to reach. In the body-obsessed world we seem to live in, we all at times feel the pressure to want to transform ourselves into perfect physical specimens. But in addition to the physical benefits of running, there are the huge boosts it gives us mentally. As we've heard in many of the stories in the book, the feel-good factor that running gives us and the way it can recharge and refresh our tired minds is a reason why so many people love running.

Think back to where you were at mentally before you started running and ask yourself these questions, scoring yourself from 1-10, 1 being 'not at all' and 10 being 'very':

How positive was your natural state of mind?
How mentally energised were you?
How able were you to cope with the daily challenges of life?
How confident did you feel?
How relaxed did you feel?

Once you have done this exercise, go through the same questions, but this time, scoring yourself in terms of how you feel now having started running. You should already be able to see the improvements you've made to your mental health. Running is a great outlet for the stresses of life and generally makes us much better able to cope with the difficulties that we all experience. We all need ways to vent this stress, and running along with exercises, meditation and so on, make sure that we are venting our stresses in ways that benefit our health rather than increasing our anxieties.

Measure your physical progress

Although running isn't all about the physical benefits, for some people, this is an important reason why they take it up and keep motivated. There are many good ways to gauge your physical progress. Following are a few things you can do to measure your progress so far. It is useful to keep a record of these measurements so that you can refer back to them and see the progression over time.

Look at yourself

Probably the most blindingly obvious way to spot changes in your body is to look at yourself. Looking back at photos is probably an even more reliable way to see changes than looking in the mirror. Mainly because when we look in the mirror, we are only ever seeing a day's worth of difference. If you are brave enough, keep your own record of photos of yourself so you can check back on progress. In all likelihood, other people will probably see the changes before you do and let you know in the way of compliments.

Measure your body fat

You can buy callipers and charts very cost-effectively online that will enable you to measure your body fat percentage. I much prefer this as a method for measuring body weight than weighing yourself on scales. Mainly because scales don't take into account the muscle mass that you will have gained from running. This is also why BMI as a form of measurement is massively flawed when determining fat weight versus muscle weight.

Recalculate your biological age

You'll recall the walking test from Chapter 1 that we used to calculate your biological age. Now would be a great time to redo this test and see how many years you have knocked off your age score from before. This is a great exercise to do every six months or so because I can guarantee that if you are running regularly, you will be able to knock many years off your biological age in a matter of months.

Set new goals

Goals play an important part in maintaining motivation in any training program, and running is no exception. What these goals are will be very personal to you and will likely evolve over time. Maybe you want to improve your stamina, lose weight or improve your mental health. Whatever it is, you should take the time to acknowledge your achievements and set new targets for yourself.

I find I'm very motivated by pushing myself to try different types of running events and also by trying to beat my own times over certain distances. For me, the physical benefits are a by-product of an activity that gives me a focus and also helps me to manage anxiety and stress. For you, it will likely be something completely different.

Every few months, it is a good idea to look back at what you have enjoyed about running. Ask yourself what has given you the biggest sense of achievement and what would you still like to achieve. This will help guide you in creating new goals for yourself that will likely give you the most enjoyment as well as the biggest sense of achievement.

I would encourage you to challenge yourself with your goals. When I signed up for my first half marathon, I was terrified. And I felt the same when I signed up to do a full marathon. But these are decisions I'm so glad that I made. Try and do at least one event that will push you outside your comfort zone once a year. When you start taking this approach, it's amazing how quickly what were once huge challenges can become things you can do relatively comfortably. This means your comfort zone has gotten bigger, which in turn means so must your ambition.

CONCLUSION

The end without an ending

I would like to end this book by hoping that there is no ending to your running adventures. There isn't a blueprint or body type for the perfect runner – if you run, then you are a runner. It doesn't matter how or where you choose to do it. And as we've heard within the stories in the previous pages, running is something that can be done by anyone and at any age.

As Eileen Noble said in her account, 'If you can walk, then you can run. It's the same but a bit quicker.'. There is a simplicity to this statement that I love. In the age of real-time stats, it can be easy to overcomplicate running, but it's something that doesn't actually require any expensive equipment or even a special place to do it. Most of us are fortunate enough to have the freedom to run wherever we like, and whenever we like – we simply have to lace up and go.

In life, there are always barriers to be overcome. Often, we see these barriers as negative, things that are blocking our way. But it's also possible to flip the perspective and see them as challenges from which we can gain positive learning experiences.

If we look back to the chapter on the age barrier, we can clearly see that age doesn't have to get in the way of our physical ambitions. If you put in the work, you can still be achieving incredible endurance feats right through your later years. People like Eileen and Ais prove this and show how we can all wind back our biological clocks by persistently maintaining and building our fitness as we age. Running is a fantastic way to boost our aerobic exercise which, as we've learnt, can reduce our biological ages by several decades. The proof is there that at any age, we can reset and reverse the clock on our biological age.

In Chapter 2, we've also seen how being unfit doesn't have to stand in the way of us taking up exercise. Whatever your current view of your own physical image, it's worth reiterating that no one looks good running. We all end up covered in sweat and pulling funny faces, which is a great equaliser. Put simply, we are all in the same boat, and we all need to start somewhere. This, along with the fact that runners are a real mix of shapes, sizes, and abilities, is probably why the running community is so open-minded and non-judgemental. Above all, it's important to remember that you are on your personal fitness journey and that you are doing this for yourself, no one else. If you can harness this powerful internal drive, then just like Roger Wright, you can overcome your inner doubts to go on and achieve whatever you set your mind to.

Even when it comes to severe barriers such as illness, it doesn't mean that we have to just give up. Everyone will get sick to a greater or lesser degree at some stage in their life. These illnesses always mark a turning point, but which direction you take from these points depends upon the mindset that you apply to your recovery. Ais's account of her battles with many illnesses shows us that every setback can become an opportunity to review, rebuild, and refocus our goals.

We've seen in Chapter 4 how the invisible challenges of mental health can be isolating and energy-draining but also how they can be overcome. As I have learnt, if you are willing to push yourself outside your comfort zone and make your world a bit bigger every day, then you can push your anxiety right into the background of your life. Running is an amazing way to manage anxiety, depression and many other mental health conditions. Simply filling the lungs with fresh air and raising your heart rate will burn nervous energy and boost your mental wellbeing. And by taking positive action, we regain control of our lives.

The time barrier is probably the most commonly used excuse as to why people don't exercise more. And quite understandably. Our lives are busier than ever with much more work time and much less leisure time. But as Delores talked about in her account, we can see that even as a busy mother, it is possible to carve out the time in crammed schedules for running and self-care. This can be essential in refuelling the body to cope with the demands. Exercise uses energy, but it also gives us energy.

In Chapter 6, we heard how tiredness and exhaustion can be big barriers to running. Both physical and mental fatigue can impact how often we exercise and how productive that exercise is. And running alone doesn't get rid of tiredness from your life, but it is guaranteed to increase your energy levels and flood your body with feel-good endorphins. And if people like Marlene Lowe can overcome M.E/CFS to run, then for the rest of us, our daily-life tiredness is certainly something we can beat.

Imagine a life without any obstacles; how dull and flat would that be? Our greatest achievements can often come off the back of our greatest obstacles. So really, we should see all these barriers more like levels in a computer game; things to be outsmarted and overcome so that we can progress onwards and upwards.

Running is a lifelong journey of discovery. I'm still finding new ways to challenge myself as well as finding out more about my physical and mental limits. Fitness is always going to be a work in progress, but as long as it is working and progressing, that's all that really matters.

I sincerely hope that the examples, advice, and actions within this book give you the confidence to overcome your own barriers to running. Whatever it may be that's been holding you back, know that it's possible to move past this to embrace a better physical version of yourself. It won't always be easy, there will be setbacks, but the important thing is to keep trying.

All that's left now is for me to wish you an abundance of strength, energy, and happiness as you imprint your own personal running story into the pavements, fields, and mountains of the world.

EPILOGUE

The mountain marathon
(that never happened)

When I started writing this book, it was a couple of months before the Covid-19 pandemic hit the planet. At that point, I had a full plan of races plotted through the year, with the ultimate challenge being the Snowdonia Mountain Half Marathon. I imagined an account of this would mark a fitting finale to my own running story.

But then the pandemic arrived, and all races were cancelled and put on hold.

Looking back now, I think that during this time I've actually learnt more about motivation and training than any mountain marathon could teach me. This last year has been one of the toughest that the world has known economically, socially, and physically. In our family, we tragically lost my father-in-law to Covid-19, and my wife is also still recovering from the effects of Long Covid. There's so much that is still unknown about this disease, and it will be a long time before its impact on our physical health and mental health is fully understood.

What is certain is that the pandemic has magnified just about every barrier that is mentioned in this book. But I still believe that the practices and advice set out in each chapter are more relevant than ever. And with physical health playing a huge part in the survival rates for this cruel disease, there's never been a more critical time for us all to try and improve our fitness and give our immune systems the very best shot.

With only virtual races to train for and the normal community of runners being forced into isolation, the standard structures and support that many people use as motivation have all but vanished. It's been much harder for us all to maintain the discipline of exercise and find the time for self-care, but I know for me that running has been a real tonic for the challenges of the last twelve months.

In a way, everyone has had to climb their own mountain this year. I'm hoping that for us all, the clouds soon start to clear and that we can enjoy a brighter outlook once more.

BIBLIOGRAPHY AND REFERENCES

[1]holmesplace.com-medical-slowing-metabolism-bodies-30s

[2]sciencedaily.com-releases

[3]Stroud, Mike. Survival Of The Fittest. Random House. Kindle Edition

[4]runnersworld.com-effect-of-ageing-on-endurance

[5]independent.co.uk-age-biology-health

[6]wikipedia.org-VO2-max

[7]sparkpeople.com-fitness

[8]verywellfit.com-rockport-fitness-walking-test

[9]lifestyle-gymtimidation-study

[10]ukrunchat.co.uk

[11]lonelygoat.com

[12]runnersworld.com-muscle-memory-injury

[13]Brigid Schulte, Overwhelmed, Bloomsbury Paperbacks, 2015

[14]Timothy Ferriss, The 4-hour work week, Vermilion, 2011

[15]rescuetime.com-busyness-paradox

[16]tandfonline.com

[17]Alex Hutchinson, Endure, HarperCollins, 2019

[18]themighty.com

[19]wikipedia.org-10K_run

[20]nbcnews.com-your-brain-watching-sport

ACKNOWLEDGEMENT

Firstly, I'd like to send my heartfelt gratitude to all the contributors to this book; Ais North, Eileen Noble, Delores Durko, Roger Wright and Marlene Lowe. Without your contributions, this book simply wouldn't have been possible. You were all so generous with your time, and the honesty of your accounts really inspired me to do your stories justice. I'd like to thank my wife Sat for her constant encouragement as I worked away on the book, and my son Otis for his patience. And I'd also like to thank my parents for their continued support through good and bad times and for instilling in me the self-belief to get things started, as well as the work ethic to get things done.

ABOUT THE AUTHOR

Clint Adam Lovell

Clint has been a keen amateur runner for over a decade. In that time, he has experienced the many benefits that running has brought to his own physical and mental health and has been inspired by the stories of how it has helped other people. He is a qualified Level 2 Fitness Instructor and is currently completing his Level 3 Personal Trainer and Nutritional Therapist qualifications. For his day job, Clint works as a Creative Director for a London advertising agency and has over 20 years of experience in the creative industry. He is married with one son and lives in Hampshire within running distance of the beautiful countryside of Southern England.

Printed in Great Britain
by Amazon